A SETH BOOK

THE EARLY CLASS SESSIONS

Book 4

by Jane Roberts

Sessions
5/25/71 to 1/25/72

A NOTE ABOUT "THE CLASS SESSIONS" & THE SETH AUDIO COLLECTION

The Seth "Class Session" books will cover Seth sessions held in Jane Roberts "ESP" Class from 1967 to the end of January 1972. These classes were held prior to the recordings used in The Seth Audio Collection.

The Seth Audio collection recordings begin, in general, in 1972. These are actual recordings of Seth speaking during Jane's class in Elmira NY which are being published in CD format along with written transcripts. There are 39 CD's already issued and more will be forthcoming. The Seth Audio Collection will cover the Seth sessions held in Jane Roberts ESP Classes from 1972 -1979, with the exception of some classes for which we do not possess a recording.

THE EARLY SESSIONS

The Early Sessions consist of the first 510 sessions dictated by Seth through Jane Roberts. There are 9 books in *The Early Sessions* series.

THE PERSONAL SESSIONS

The Personal Sessions, often referred to as "the deleted sessions," are Seth sessions that Jane Roberts and Rob Butts considered to be of a highly personal nature and were therefore kept in separate notebooks from the main body of the Seth material. *The Personal Sessions* are published in 7 volumes.

NEW AWARENESS NETWORK INC.
P.O. BOX 192 , MANHASSET, N.Y. 11030

WWW. SETHCENTER.COM

A SETH BOOK

THE EARLY CLASS SESSIONS

Book 4

by Jane Roberts

Sessions
5/25/71 to 1/25/72

© 2010 by Laurel Davies Butts

Published by New Awareness Network Inc.

New Awareness Network Inc.
P.O. Box 192
Manhasset, New York 11030

Opinions and statements on health and medical matters expressed in this book are those of the author and are not necessarily those of or endorsed by the publisher. Those opinions and statements should not be taken as a substitute for consultation with a duly licensed physician.

Cover Design: Michael Goode
Editorial: Rick Stack
Typography: Raymond Todd, Michael Goode

All rights reserved. This book may not be reproduced in whole or in part, without written permission from the publisher, except by a reviewer who may quote brief passages in a review; nor may any part of this book be reproduced, stored in a retrieval system, or transmitted in any form or by any means electronic, mechanical, photocopying, recording, or other, without written permission from the publisher.

ISBN 978-0-9768978-8-0
Printed in U.S.A.

I dedicate The Class Sessions
*to my wife, Jane Roberts,
who lived her 55 years
with the greatest creativity
and the most valiant courage.*

-Robert F. Butts, Jr.

ESP CLASS SESSION, MAY 25, 1971
TUESDAY

(The group went into Alpha I and gave their impressions. Theodore made a remark about a friend.)

He is a delightful peacock.

(A discussion of Brady's impressions of Theodore. Discussion of the origins of Heaven and Hell followed.)

Now I want you all to know, and it will please you no end, that you have an authority present, for I was a pope in 300 AD. I was not a very good pope.

([Theodore:] "Shall we kiss your ring?")

I am sorry, I do not have it here, and I will not make any suitable comments that Ruburt might make, following your statement.

However, there is something that you should know. Because you are physically oriented, you early got it into your heads that goodness must have a place in the physical universe and evil must have a place within it. And so you set up for yourselves the division of Heaven and Hell. In one story or another, it has existed far back into the annals of your time. Now give us a moment.

As I have tried to explain to you, the rigorous concepts of good and evil are themselves highly distorted, and when you find such a dilemma where goodness is one thing and evil another, and both contrary and separate, then you automatically separate them in your minds and in your feelings and in your fantasies. You do not seem at this point able to realize that what you call evil works for what you call good, or that both are a part of energy, and that you are using energy to form your reality, both now and after this life. This is because you deal with effects physically, as you see them. And until you divest yourself of such psychological behavior, it will always seem to you that good and evil are opposites, and you will treat them as such in your feelings and in your concepts and in your myths.

([Ron L:] "Is it ever justified to do evil for the sake of good?")

In the terms in which you ask the question, the answer is no.

([Ron:] "In other words, in this reality we are faced with decisions in this context, is it true that our decisions can be only constructive and good or destructive and evil?")

Only in the terms in which you ask the question. In larger terms, there is no such thing as destruction; and your second question does not follow logically from the first one. Now if you will look at the script when you receive it, you will see what I mean. You ask questions without considering the answers that have been given. Think of the answers before you form your next question.

([Ron:] "Yes, but I don't necessarily agree with the logic of your answers.")

I do not need you to agree with my logic. I need you to understand the faulty quality in your own logic, and

SESSION 5/25/1971

that must come from yourself and not from me. Now, wait. Part of this is due to the fact that you form questions before you comprehend the nature of the answers that you have received. Read the script. Find out the answers I have given you, and then form your questions.

([Ron. :] "Well, I have a question that I know I'm going to form after I read the script, and that is that your response was that my question was only meaningful in the terms that I use. So for you, how do you conceive of good and evil in your own reality?")

There is no destruction and there *is* no evil. But while you believe that there is, then you must act accordingly. While you believe that to murder a man is to destroy his consciousness forever, then you cannot murder, and in your terms it is an evil.

([Ron:] "Well, Hitler could have used that justification for wiping out 9 million Jews.")

He could have, indeed.

([Ron:] "Well then I have to disagree with you. I think that even in the way we look at it now that there is destruction, which is evil...")

I know that you do. You live within that reality, and while you live within it, you must deal with it, and so you are.

([Ron:] "Is there such a thing as a moral decision for someone who exists in the next plane of existence?")

There are always moral decisions. They involve the use of creativity and development. They involve the use of spontaneity.

([Ron:] "What system of values do you use to choose in your moral decisions?")

I have told you. My last answer implies that answer.

(Ron:) "In your words, it would be whatever is the most creative in terms of what you want to do."

We will ignore the last part of your sentence and agree with the first part. And I shall certainly see to it, if I have any abilities to do so, that in your next life, you are put in the position of answering someone whose mind works exactly as yours does.

(To Brady.) Now. Here we have creative love and intelligence operating this evening spontaneously and creatively in making contact with another. This is what you should learn to achieve.

([Ron:] "I feel like I've made contact with you very well.")

You have, indeed. However, the intuitive rapport that you need to contact others within your environment is at least to some extent lacking. Reach out to them with feeling, rather than with the guise of probing words.

([Ron:] "I don't necessarily deal with physical entities the same way I'm dealing with you right now.")

You should learn to. Now. We will take a break.

(To Theodore.) Active peace in your direction over there and be glad that you aroused the sort of response in our friend here *(Brady)* that you did. It was good for both of you.

(After break.)

(To Ron) I egg—listen to me—I egg you on. It is

good for you and good for the class and very good for this one over here *(Florence)*, because you ask questions that she is already thinking of, and for some reason she has suddenly grown timid about her questions. Now, continue.

([Ron:] "I was just saying that no evil can be justified on the basis of the greater good.")

That is what I told you operates within your reality, and you did not listen to my answer. When you read the text, it will be simply clarified. In your reality, the stance that you adapt is a necessary one, and you must hold to it. The fact that it does only apply to your system need not presently concern you.

([Ron:] "Are there instances in which a spirit from another reality would intervene in this reality, and we would call that a destructive act, but the spirit would say it was creative?")

Not. *(Pause)* I do not like your term. Now. Any such intervention would only occur on the part of a personality who was, for the present time, physical. As indeed mentioned last week, the villain in a religious drama would be a creative figure. But he would exist historically in your time and not, for example, be a ghost whispering in the night. There are no creatures whispering evil in your ear.

([Ron:] "There are no entities intervening?")

Not in those terms.

(Ron:) "But in the terms that we are all spirits acting out our own inner drama, the term spirit has some meaning?")

Sometimes, but only occasionally, I think you are catching on.

(During break, Ron got into a discussion with Brady about good and evil and forces involved.)

No! There are no forces outside of yourselves that in your terms cause you to do evil. Unfortunately, what you think of as good and evil reside within yourselves, and you cannot blame an evil force for the destruction that runs rampant across the earth. Again, in your terms, these are your problems, and no god or devil put them upon you, and there is no one to blame but yourselves. On the other hand, for the seasons and the idiot flower *(looks at Joel H.)*, you have yourselves to thank. You are learning how to use the creative energy of which you are a part, and you are indeed quite isolated, so you cannot do much harm, in your terms. And so that the evil that you think you do is an illusion. And so that for the millions that you think you slay, you slay not one. And so that despite you and your concepts of value, creativity always emerges triumphant, and those that are killed in one war come back to fight against war the next time, and hopefully, you teach yourselves some lessons. And if you destroy your planet, you will have others to work with, and those that were destroyed are not destroyed. You are in a training system. The mistakes in the long run, and in your terms, will not count, but they are very real to you at this time.

(During break, a discussion of Seth's life as a pope.)

I had two illegitimate children *(laughter)*, a mistress

that sneaked into my private studies, a magician that I kept in case I did not do too well on my own, a housekeeper who was pregnant every year that I had her, and three daughters who joined a nunnery because I would not have them, and I am referred to in barely three paltry lines, for my reign did not last very long. Now, I had a large family, that is, I came from a large family. And I was ambitious, as all intelligent young men of that time were. I did not go for the military, and so there was nothing to do but go to the Church.

Now. For a while I was not in Rome, but held my religious call elsewhere. I wrote two Church laws. It should all go to show you that some good ends up from everything. I died of trouble with my stomach because I was such a glutton. My name was not Clement *(to Theodore)*, though Clement is a lovely name. I was originally called Protonius. Now give me a moment. The last name is not nearly so clear, and this is not my papal name, but my, if you will forgive the term, common name. Meglemanius. The third. From a small village. Unless I summon the self that I was at that time, the memories for details are not that clear. But as I now recall them, without directly checking on our friend the pope, who has, you must understand, gone his own way, I am coming as close as I can. We did not have as many guards at that time, but we had many stolen paintings and jewels of great merit. Now some of these jewels, as well as the money, went for expeditions that you do not realize were adopted at that time, having to do with commerce and ships sent through Africa, and this interest had to do with my later life when I was involved with the oregano. My sniffing goes back for centuries.

There were two brothers strongly united in control of Italy at the time. Perhaps I should say two males, one in the higher capacity and the other his chancellor, with whom I was involved as pope. And I sent armies to the north also.

We had not yet begun the strong insistence upon indulgences *(looks at Brady)*, so I did not have that extra cash that indulgences would bring in. *(To Theodore)* I believed and did not believe, as you earlier believed and did not believe, and did a good job of hiding from myself what I believed and what I did not believe. And the higher one gets in power, the harder it is to hide such things from one's self.

I was very fond of my first mistress, whose name was Maria. And there were no such sane rules as those in which you now sit. And there were no governments as secure in which you could reside as those you now enjoy. I did believe implicitly in the God in which I was brought up, and in that belief. It was only later that I wondered how such a God would choose me for such a position and then I began to wonder. I had four lives following that of the most adverse circumstances to make sure that I understood the difference between luxury and poverty, pride and compassion. And there were days that I walked in other centuries the same streets that I had walked as a pope, but then only put my fancy toes abruptly upon and lifted them up again. But as a peasant I walked with a heavy foot and great weight until I learned the lessons that I had to learn, as all of you will learn your own lessons.

(To Natalie.) Now, I will help you send energy to your tree. If we can fix one tree, surely we can do something with the universe.

(During break, discussion of what class had done during the week.)

(To Ron) Now, if you would pay attention, you could wake up in a dream and understand me more clearly.

(To group.) And all of you attend the classes of which you frequently remember your experiences, and I expect even more frequent memory on your part as time goes by. A particularly important class will be held later this evening. And I even expect you *(Ron)* to remember the dream.

(To Brady.) And you will be a guest, if you do not mind cavorting with past popes. I know it is against your principles, but then it is against my own *(laughter)*. A past pope is better than a present one.

CLASS QUIZ I

(Author: Susan M. Watkins)
1. According to the Seth Material, one chair is perceived by 5 people as

a) 50 chairs
b) 12 marigolds
c) invisible
d) a lump of coal
e) none of the above

2. You ask Seth about life. He says
a) "that's how it goes"
b) "The answer is the sound of one hand clapping"
c) "Who cares?"
d) "Go away"
e) all of the above

3. Seth says the childlike self is
a) out in the yard
b) uneducated
c) too loud
d) wet
e) b, c, and d

4. Physical reality is
a) a porcelain sink
b) haphazard
c) two flights up
d) terminal
e) in the key of G

5. Karma is
a) 10 cents a pound
b) a harmless untruth
c) sold by Avon
d) the swordswallower at the fair
e) some of the above

CLASS QUIZ I

6. You tell class about a dream. Seth says
   a) "the answer lies within"
   b) "the answer lies within"
   c) "the answer lies within"
   d) "the answer lies within"
   e) none of the above
7. Seth calls Jane
   a) Arnold
   b) Sam
   c) Flipper
   d) at night
   e) on an FM frequency
8. There is no one in class named
   a) Harold
   b) Ralph
   c) Zelda
   d) Seth
   e) Bilbo
9. When Jane comes out of trance, who tells first?
   a) Jane
   b) Theodore
   c) Sue
   d) Gert
   e) Willie
10. A parable is
    a) ridiculous
    b) embarrassing
    c) dull
    d) a bestseller

e) obscure
11. Probable selves
  a) react to class
  b) react to suggestion
  c) react to litmus paper
  d) overreact
  e) watch TV on Tuesday nights
12. Dream objects are
  a) Freudian
  b) a dime a dozen
  c) commended by Good Housekeeping
  d) confusing
  e) rabid
13. That man in the back room is really
  a) an FBI agent
  b) running in place
  c) taking movies of the john
  d) Daniel Berrigan
  e) stoned
14. Seth ends class by biding us all a fond
  a) good morning
  b) good Friday
  c) good grief
  d) good vs. evil
  e) good riddance
15. Jane calls break
  a) too infrequently
  b) when it's her turn
  c) to set up the projector

CLASS QUIZ I

   d) whether or not Seth does
   e) to find out what's going on
16. Alpha I is useful
   a) in case of fire
   b) after every meal
   c) at cocktail parties
   d) to monks
   e) to car thieves
17. We all come to class to
   a) drink
   b) get good gossip
   c) chew oregano
   d) think about each others' bodies
   e) lie around on the floor
18. Hornets are
   a) our brothers
   b) our sisters
   c) our mothers-in-law
   d) revelationary
   e) reactionary
19. Time is
   a) a Bernard Baruch watch
   b) available by subscription only
   c) irresponsible
   d) Peoria, Illinois
   e) 5 a.m. Wednesday
20. A legitimate experience is
   a) funny
   b) weird

c) sexy
d) against the law
e) any old thing

Answer True or False:
1. Seth is speaking in his normal tone of voice.
2. There is a cat in the bathroom
3. Plants do not drink wine.
4. Sally has a detailed filing system.
5. We all enjoy sharing secrets.
6. We are all agents of the devil.
7. Suggestion plays a bigger role than Piasano.
8. We are figments of each others' disturbed imaginations.
9. Jane keeps the Shockmobile phone number handy.
10. Yesterday was Seth's birthday.

ESP CLASS SESSION, JUNE 1, 1971
TUESDAY

([Joel:] "It was war. It was the instinct to survive. They moved in and everybody could have coexisted together but it just didn't work that way. We were proud . We lived in a beautiful, but in the sense that this world has plenty, that there was nothing there. We lived and lived successfully. There were hard times. There was summer and there was famine and there were some pretty bad winters, but we were a success. We had been on that land a long time and then you people came in

and looked down on us. You thought we were a bunch of savages and you wouldn't be friends with us or talk to us. You didn't want to talk to us—we were a bunch of animals yet you lived in hovels made out of dirt. You held yourselves up and thought you were so great and inadvertently or intentionally you began to destroy us at first and then it became more of a pattern because then you sensed that your survival was hinging on it too. Then it became kind of a guerilla warfare on both sides and it accelerated. It wasn't necessary at all, but I guess we didn't know that then."

([Jane:] "You didn't even know at that time?"

([Joel:] "I just saw a hatchet kind of a thing with feathers and stuff on it and as the symbol developed it changed into a boomerang with feathers on it."

(Jane:] "Why do you think now that you try to help people that are in trouble, on the downside?"

([Joel:] "Well, it's not this one reincarnational period, I'm sure, and today I still think the Indians had and have a better life philosophy, a purer kind of thing."

([Joel to Bette:] "Do you have any feelings of what you were doing there? Why would you go where you didn't belong. You knew you didn't belong there the minute you saw the place."

([Bette:] "I didn't know I didn't belong there and I didn't really care about the Indians. All I cared about was my own."

([Joel:] "But you didn't care if the Indians lived or died or survived or moved out or what happened?"

([Bette:] "Right. I just didn't care as long as there was..."

([Joel:]) "Yet you had gone in and pushed them out of their own land."

([Bette:]) "That's right."

([Joel:]) "You knew that Indian men and women and children were dying. Didn't that affect you at all? Didn't you care?"

([Bette:]) "I didn't know at the time what was actually going on and I don't think..."

([Joel:]) "It was the only news that there was. We weren't getting any news from back East. The only gossip was whose crop failed or whose cow had a ..."

([Bette:]) "All we knew was who was on the warpath and when."

([Joel:]) "Which race are you talking about? Did you know when your people were on the warpath?"

([Bette:]) "No. I was in my own little existence. All I cared about were my own kids and you took care of that."

([Joel:]) "How about our husband?"

([Bette:]) "I didn't give a damn about him."

([Joel:]) "It just seems that you are awfully quick to condemn. After all the first blood let that day was not ours."

([Bette:]) "That day?"

([Joel:]) "That day."

([Bette:]) "Well, who started it? I sure didn't. My kids sure didn't and my husband didn't. He couldn't do anything."

([Joel:]) "Who killed the first human being?"

([Bette:]) "I don't know. Do you?"

([Joel:]) "Evidently someone..."

([Bette:]) "Well, who did then?"

SESSION 6/1/1971

([Joel:] "When we were coming in there was one guy who wasn't alive when we got there."

([Bette:] "Coming in where?"

([Joel:] "Coming in, closing in, riding up to..."

([Bette:] "To my little old mud shack? Perhaps by the time you got there I had already killed my husband."

([Joel:] "Somebody did."

([Bette:] "Well, I did. And I would do it again."

([Jane:] "She also took the first shot at you guys, but that didn't mean much because you were going to kill them anyway."

([Bette:] "Because he started to—He just didn't have any gumption to him. He started to whimper and to cry when he knew that he had his home and his family to protect and he didn't do it, and I had crying kids and I didn't need a crying husband because the older kids could shoot much better than their father because he didn't know how to pull the trigger. He didn't know how to do anything."

(Jane asked Sue if she was in it.

(Sue replied: "No."

([Jane to Bette:] "Do you know your husband now?"

([Bette:] "I don't think so, but maybe I do."

([Bette to Joel:] "Don't fight with me either. Just be nice."

([Joel:] "You said it's all over, and you don't feel that dislike anymore."

([Bette:] "Right."

([Joel:] "How about if you met your husband sometime in this life. Would you feel the same kind of forgiving spirit for

him and acceptance for him that you seem to for me now? Now that you are working it all out and letting it out now?"

([Bette:] "Yes. I learned a lot from that lifetime because I am a regular crusader when it comes to Indians and it's a wonder I haven't grabbed a sword and said, 'charge', because I have great feelings for the Indians. I have had more fights when there has been racial talks and discussions on the blacks and the whites and so on. Somehow I always managed to get the Indian into the argument so evidently I have forgiven all that they did to me until l saw Joel, and then it all came back."

([Jane:] "How do you feel towards Joel?"

([Bette:] "I feel all right. I felt fine towards Joel the first night because the minute you started talking, for weeks I had been coming to class, when I would see the war paint on him I would get a terrible pain in my head. I remarked several times in class about I had this pain in my head, and I couldn't work it out no matter what I did. And that night here in the room when you were talking it was like somebody was pulling something out of my head, and I have not had this pain or this pressure since."

([Jane:] "What about you, Joel? I don't feel it's resolved."

([Joel:] "I have to do it at a couple of levels. Intellectually first."

([Jane:] "Yes, you've only done it at a pretty surface level.

([Joel:] "Well, it may be completely resolved on all levels but you recognize the intellectual first anyway."

Jane asked Sue.

([Sue:] "I had a feeling when you first started getting

those impressions on her that I was in on this in some capacity. I have a feeling that I was only about 2 years old or other and that they got the kids last, or at least me, and I have the feeling that the house was pretty much on fire. For some reason I don't have any feelings of animosity. I don't think as a child I knew anything that was involved that was going on. I think this is why I can't stand yelling."

([Jane:] "I suggest for now we will let it ride although I don't think we have really gone all the way out of it. I don't think we got it all. I think maybe you'll move to get rid of the emotions that I sense you've got."

([Bill, an entity channeled by Joel H.:] "Part of letting it ride was what caused the difficulty in the first place and the yelling was a release of emotion and we have met before. Someone has been helping you to get over some feelings in the (night) lifetime and they are much more worked through than you might realize at the intellectual level. The advice is good. Continue probing, but what has been need not continue to be for you at this time. And since this is a night when the process of telling secrets continues, let me tell one, I have been here before.")

ESP CLASS SESSION, JUNE 8, 1971
TUESDAY

(Jane's impressions to Bette of a past life the class had

received the previous week in Alpha: "You had seven children. Your last name was something like Masar. There may be either a Y or an E at the end of it. Not the end of it. I received the impression of your absolute hatred of your husband that rushed through you at that time that had just evolved in terror. You shot him."

(During class Davey related some of his experiences while training as a parapsychologist. Seth came through, speaking to Davey.)

Now over here we have great energy, and because I am aware of your conversations, strong power that is being withheld out of caution and fear. You have a strong core of energy tested too early and not under the best of circumstances, though at the time you may have believed so. You are much easier now, but at the time, there was an explosion of energy on your part that you did not understand, and you were afraid that in this explosion of energy you would go too far outward and there would be nothing left, so to speak, that you would get away from yourself and lose yourself beyond all hopes of recovery.

Now regardless of what you may think, consciously, the hypnosis experiments did, indeed, upset you, and part of you regarded them as coercion and this you highly resented so that you sent a part of yourself where the other part of yourself did not want to go. And so you went but with faltering steps. You were enthralled, as you are enthralled, but you were underneath much more cautious.

Now we have here, for all of your benefit, some

examples, both here *(Davey)* and here *(Mary Ellen)* and here *(Joel)* of one particular phenomena. Out of humility I do not speak of myself.

(To Mary Ellen.) Now of the three cases mentioned, the greatest sense of stability and peace has been reached over here. The personality, therefore, has gone along well, and the process has been very slow. It will build.

(To Davey.) Now here we have a too early blooming of abilities before the overall personality was able to handle them, and we also have a great contrast in attitude for we have on one hand the determination to show up all fraud, and on the other hand, the fear underneath that our own experiences could somehow be fraudulent. And, therefore, you could not trust yourself and found yourself unable to continue. The dilemma came, therefore, and you avoided the field of endeavor.

Now Ruburt did not know what he was going to speak about this evening and half of his talk in class is automatic, as you know, but it was no coincidence that he became involved in his talk of power and energy for you had a deep distrust of your own energy to sway people as a salesman *(to Davey)* as you had a distrust of your ability to sway people as a minister *(to Joel)* and as you also have the same feeling *(to Davey)*, for what happens is this.

If you can sway others so easily then what is there to them after all, for you know who you are and what you are and you do not think you are all that great. If they listen to you like sheep, then how can you look to them with respect? How can you think they are worth saving? How are they worth what you want to give or can give? They are not worth the while. This is what you think when you put out this fine energy to sell a product *(to Davey)* and this is what you think *(to Joel)*. Whether or not you realize it, your conception of the human race changes, for if you can mold another that easily then where are these fine abilities inherent in the race as a whole.

You do not trust those that you can sway. You trust an adversary because you cannot move him; and you think, there is a man, he will not listen to me, therefore, he must really be great, and you also feared him, and that is why you trust your enemies in a strange fashion for they convince you that a portion of the race is worth saving. Those that stand against you, you feel have a great energy and a great power.

Now I am speaking, in your terms, for I understand the way that you feel. I have felt that way many times myself. I have also, however, been one of the ignorant masses, in your terms, who listened to the ringing through the centuries. I have been taken in by every kind of con game that the centuries have known and what you have forgotten is that so have you. You have been on both sides of the fence. You are learning to know what energy is and how to use it. Now you are on one side of the fence, in your terms, but you have been on the other sides."

(To Joel.) And you have been a poor, ignorant, stu-

pid ignoramus that now you are trying to reach.

(To Ron L.) I am not looking for questions, but you have been the emotional mother that you are now trying to forget, and you have been swept by those emotions that you are now afraid to release, and you have felt them as a river and have been afraid of where they would lead you.

Now, again, each of you have available to you the energy that sweeps through this frame. You can use it in whatever way you choose, but you will use it, and you use it every moment that you are alive and every moment that, in your terms, you are not alive. You are using it creatively whether you know it or not, and it shouts through you even though you purse your lips, and it speaks through you even though you tense your muscles to hide it. Therefore, it behooves you to become friends with it.

(As Jane came out of trance, Gert remarked that Seth had thrown her glasses.)

I did it for our friend over here. I do it for several reasons because it is an excellent display of the use of energy and because it is fun, because it is active peace and because it shows you that the dead can be more livelier than those who think they are alive. And also to show you that the ego structure is not completely annihilated.

(Joel told Jane that Seth had tapped him on the toes with her glasses.)

It is a gesture showing my exuberance. It is not always appreciated, but I can make a lovelier *(word lost)* and, as my close friends here know, it is also a very simple demonstration to show you that I am not a spooky old spirit at all. And that the emotions survive the body of which you are so proud.

(To Davey.) I will turn around so that you can see me better, and now I will return to our friend Ruburt, and you are welcome to our class.

(During break a discussion of Joel's, Mary Ellen's and Davey's abilities and some felt they had not progressed very much.)

I am not finished with you, I was simply speaking in terms of one particular phenomena. I did not mean that others did not have strong abilities. These were simply examples of one case in point.

This is only a preliminary and you *(Joel)* and you *(Davey)* will be here for the rest of it, for I am only dealing with your attitudes and emotions at this stage and as you understand them. There is far more to it than that, and there are reasons for your feelings that you do not as yet understand.

Now I must make myself friendly to our two young ladies over here, and say good evening to you so that you will not think that I am some spooky thing that comes in the night.

([Guest:] "You have made that quite clear.")

I am glad, I certainly try.

You should also know that nothing in our classes goes unrecognized or unrecorded in other layers of actuality beside those of which you know.

(To Ron L.) So if it makes you uptight to know that

transcripts of our sessions go to New York, it will doubtlessly make you even more uptight to realize the transcripts go to places that have no names and take up no space. I will put in a word for you. I will see that your name is spelled correctly.

Now I will let you all take a break. I innocently said a break, meaning a Seth break, which means that I was not stepping in on our friend's territory, which is simply an "in" joke around here. Now sometime I am simply going to keep Ruburt in trance during your break, and then I will circulate among you and add my comments to yours.

([Gert:] "During psy time I got a picture, I think of myself, as a man standing in a grassy area, like someone's backyard, and a woman. There were three children. She carried one on her right hip and I would say about 18 months old, about a two year old and a five year old, and the girl had braids, and they were looped around, and she had a big apron on. I didn't see her face, but I got the feeling that she was my wife and that I was not being very compassionate or understanding to her. My question is, was this me or was it something I was picking up?")

It was in a life both in Sweden and Denmark. There were two lives. One in the 1500's or late 1400's and one in the 1700's. One as quite a cosmopolitan around Oslo. None of that material, however, has any bearing now on the specific challenges on which you are working. The lives were relatively neutral. You were picking up, however, your own feelings at that time.

Now give us a moment. You joined a navy not of your own country. I believe the English navy during one of these lives and traveled far off the north coast. You spent, also, some time in Ireland, and this is approximately now 1732 to 1750 at which time you retired. You were extremely dogmatic. Given to ceremony, again, counting your brass buttons. Working to be the equivalent of an admiral.

At the same time, however, you came into contact with merchants, quite unusual in this particular circumstance, coming up from Africa. This particular expedition was lost, and you divested the ship of its cargo with the help of the men on your ship, and of course without giving payment. <u>Alae</u> *(spelled out)*, now that was the name of a particular type of cargo, perhaps algae, that was a part of the ships contents. There was also, however, some opium from Turkey. You made a killing on the opium in Holland. It is nearly impossible to find, for example, any proof or record of that transaction since you did not deal in contracts but relied upon your word of honor. In this case it meant taking the contents of the hold by force.

You nearly ended up on the gallows in England. However, you were lucky enough to escape and spend your finer years as a contented potbellied old gentleman near Oslo. Now, the name of the town began with a B and I can only approximate it. Baenog—another letter and then oe, what you would call an outskirt of Oslo, twelve miles distant. Your last name, Bungannon. The first name, Thomas. The wife's name, Sarah. And he left

44 grandchildren and great, great grandchildren. You had 7 children in all.

(An Alpha session for the woman with multiple sclerosis.)

Now I will shortly leave you, but before I do there is something I would like you to try. First of all, listen to my voice. Use it. Attach your own energy to it also. Let the sound of its energy rouse you from your own sleeping. Let it then rouse your own energy, lift you from your sleep. Energy is not only eternal but limitless. There is no limit to the energy that is available to you. Therefore, you do not have to worry that what energy you use is, therefore, denied you in the future so open up the doors within yourselves.

Imagine, if you must, that you have backdoors through which this energy emerges, fresh from the fountains of the universe. Now imagine this universe, imagine this energy connecting; focused, vital and strong. Close your eyes and imagine it in this room. Imagine all the energy that is available to you, here now, connected and send it outward to the woman in question. Send it through space and time easily through the vehicle of my voice. Use my voice, therefore, as a vehicle upon which unending energy can rise and let that power then of vitality and life and strength enter the body and spirit and mind of the woman and fill her with the feeling of vital life and give her the knowledge of herself that she now so desperately requires. Feel that energy glide as easily through the air as air currents; as naturally and as easily as the wind that feels both night and day. Feel it then fill her frame with vitality and strength and know that you have a part in this, and that through the part that you are playing are you also being filled with therapeutic energies and with vitalities that will rejuvenate your spirit and your mind.

And leave this place then in joy and freedom and exaltation and know that you have helped another, and that through opening the doors of energy are you then filled with it and ever replenished and that through giving do you receive. And I bid you then to return to this place and this room.

And those blessings that I have to give I do, indeed, give to you, and those blessings that I do not have to give, as usual, you will have to seek on your own. And a hearty good evening to you all.

ESP CLASS SESSION, JUNE 15, 1971
TUESDAY

(Following a discussion on reincarnation.)

Now and I bid you all good evening. I have only a few comments to make, however, but everyone, including our visitors, everyone who comes here comes for a reason simply as you come together in any context for a reason. There is a reason why you have been born into this place and this time as you know it, and granting that, there is also a reason why you have come here to this room as you know it.

There are, indeed then, connections between you that you would call past connections but connections that also reach into the future as you conceive of it. You have all met each other either as strong friends or relatives or acquaintances or simply as strangers who passed each other perhaps upon a street in another time and another place. And so there is nothing strange in your coming here. You simply recognize each other, and you come together as old friends have a habit of doing, and you have a great pretense that you have not known each other before, and that the encounter is a new one. And you keep within yourself these memories buried.

(To Joel.) And you do not allow yourself to remember that the Lady of Florence was a very strong taskmaster followed by you in China in a Ching dynasty. Or that you resented him greatly. And all the intricate reasoning that you learned at that time you now hide from yourself.

(To Florence.) And those connections that you know very well, you deny.

Now these matters are open to you to a much larger degree when you are in Alpha, but I suggest that from now on you learn to utilize Alpha II where the resistances that you so nicely throw up in Alpha I will be to some extent disregarded as far as reincarnational information is concerned.

(To Sue.) Now I will tell you the full story but at another time, and if you have not already discovered it.

Now what you all do when I speak is recognize

within my own vitality your own. For as I have told you often, when I speak, I speak for you. And you can feel as an echo within my words the energy of the interior self that is your true identity. And, also if you allow it, the voice can also be used to echo other voices that have been your own in other times and places as Ruburt earlier said. And it can also be used to acquaint you with the easy release of energy that is your own, and the free spontaneous joy of expressing it.

Why do you then hamper yourselves? The freedom is yours now, as available to you as it is to me, and easier for you to use since you are more familiar with your own body than I am with Ruburt's. You direct it outward unconsciously as you go about your daily endeavors so easily and so automatically that the miracle of it escapes you. And yet, if you listen, you can hear the easy release of energy as the blood flows throughout your veins and directed outward for those purposes in which you believe.

(To Mark.) Now over here our friend, you are trying too hard and too consciously. Imagine a stream or a breeze and go along with it. You have it in your mind that there is some dam or wall that you must encounter before you are free to leave your body, and such is not the case. Allow your energy to flow freely out from you and you will flow with it.

(To Sue.) Now your friend was a jealous leader. A very good leader, but a jealous one.

([Derek:] "Is Mark's problem his trying to project? I have some problems trying to project. I have not been successful, at

least not that I know of yet, and I think of a wall too that I can't get out of."

You are afraid, and he is, unconsciously, that you will fall off the edges of the known universe, that the conscious mind won't function out of the body, and that only chaos will meet you, and this is not the case. There are some differences here between what you consciously tell yourself and what you unconsciously are afraid of and what you unconsciously believe.

If you imagine yourself as a part of energy and a part of All That Is and an identity that forms and creates your body, then you know you create it with each breath that you take. And with each portion of your thought and desire you can leave it as freely as a vagabond who can then find peace and joy and contentment in any corner of the universe and reform your body as well with joy and exaltation, and not fear it will disintegrate or disappear while you are gone.

([Derek:] "I usually get tied up with my breathing. As soon as I feel like I might be able to forget about my body, my breathing, I stop breathing, and then I worry about it.")

You are overconcentrating upon methods. Think of your purpose, and the methods will take care of themselves.

([Joel:] "I guess in the beginning Jane and Rob were a little ambivalent as to whether they wanted to go and check the Frank Withers thing, and we have not made any attempt to check the stuff that Bill gave the first time—That I, in the '40s and having been a lawyer and went to Northwestern

law school, practiced law in the Loop, that kind of thing. And Hazel last week stopped in Chicago on the way across country and got the address of the Bar Association and some other people, and we're finally going to check this stuff. But I wondered if you could give us any information as to how we might go about it, or if the initial information was accurate, or if you can tell us anything that we ought to check into in particular?")

Your problem is this. It is not important in the beginning whether or not the information checked for you were involved in the opening of new channels. To insist, therefore, that all the information be perfect, or your material has no value, is of course, a predicament that I hope you will not fall into. Do you follow me? Therefore, check the material for you will not feel happy unless you do, and then apply what I have told you. As you continue, your information will prove more and more checkable in the physical reality to which you presently ascribe, and if you are interested in that area then, indeed, it must to some extent bear a strong relationship to the reality that you know if you request it. If you demand that as part of the validity of what you are getting, then you will receive it, but do not rush. Allow yourself freedom and time. Do you follow me?

([Joel:] "Yes, I just wondered if you had any additional information perhaps that we might want to look into as we proceeded. I don't think it's the kind of thing, for example, if it doesn't check out we are not going to say, 'Well, Bill, you're a fake, go away.")

SESSION 6/15/1971

You are forming the psychological bridge. Use it and allow it to grow. The foundations of it begin in one place and end up in another. It becomes stronger as you continue, and it can be used for various things as you continue. Do not require it to carry too much weight before it is ready to. Give it time, let it grow. Now Bill will become more and more Bill, less and less like Seth, more and more like Bill and then less like Bill and more like someone else entirely different. You are on a journey. The journey creates its own destination. You have a more solid framework now than you had earlier and you have gotten over successfully several pitfalls into which you could have fallen.

(During break there was a discussion of Grace Rittenberger's method of giving life readings, especially the form letter of questions.)

And for the rest of you a far more formal framework that I should get you used to. It would do you all good. You would not stand for it, but it would do you good.

(To Mary Ellen.) I beg your pardon for the interruption.

I would not like it, but it would be a good idea for them. It would get them in shape. Tempermentally, however, I have never gone for such a framework, but I will have to think one up, it is a fine challenge. I wish to show you that after death you still have a temperment in case any of you wondered.

(To Florence.) Particularly for our Lady of Florence over here in the corner. This intellect will still be bugging

you. I want you to know it. Settle your accounts with it now, and take it along on your journeys. It is you who keep your intellect in such a closed room while your intuitions want to give it more freedom. The divisions do not exist, they are mirages.

(To Mary Ellen.) And now I do, indeed, myself apologize.

(Jane had the class go into Alpha to experience their own impressions.)

Now you have been given a small insight into the ways in which your inner memories work. You react to others, not only because of their position and relationship to you in this place and in this time, but because of memories from the past and, in your terms, because of memories from the future. For what you do today affects not only the future, in your terms, but also the past. And the words that you spoke now affect the past as you think of it, for time has open ends. Now if you think of time as a line, I do not only mean that time is open-ended at either side, you see, for time cannot be considered as a single line. Instead it goes out in all directions. The directions of which you can conceive and directions of which you cannot conceive.

You do not understand the nature of creativity and, therefore, you cannot understand the nature of time. So when I tell you that time has open ends I will presently be satisfied if you understand that you can affect both the past and the future from your present viewpoint, and that is extremely simple. The whole idea is far more complex.

Our friend, Joel, reacts to our Lady of Florence, therefore, as she appears to him now in this place and in this time, and yet he also reacts as a person that he was, in your terms, and our Lady of Florence reacts as a person she was, in your terms.

In larger terms, however, you are not only the people that you were but the people that you will be. So you are affected, again only in your terms, by your future reincarnations as well as your past ones. You can, therefore, in your present say something that will change the past. And 5000 years from now you can speak to your present selves and carry a message which you will now, in this moment, understand.

Now you can open yourselves to this reality or you can deny it. You can open yourselves in dreams and if you prefer, reveries, to these realities or close yourselves to them. You can with your mirror accept these other personalities, search them out and recognize them, or pretend that they do now exist. But this in no way denies the validity of your entire personality.

Now if you are going to understand human personality or deal with the psychology of being, then you must first of all examine your own being and you cannot examine it as you can a rock. You must become your own vehicle and travel through the realities that lie within yourselves. Travel through your own reactions to each other, and you will find the answers that seem to elude you. Follow minutely, even in class, the reactions that you have one to another, and they will lead you to inner pathways. Do not think: "this could be true, but it is fantasy." Follow it through and see what you get, and then examine it. The answers never lie outside of yourselves. They do not lie in a Bill. They do not lie in a Seth. The answers lie within Sue and Bette and Mary Ellen and Natalie and Joel. They lie within each one of you.

(During break there was a discussion of the above.

(To Arnold.) You can experience it, and then let the intellect figure out what the inner self has learned.

([Arnold:] "If our intellects are capable of it.")

They are capable of far more than you allow them to be capable of if you do not hamper them by ideas of what is possible and what is not. It was a good question. And it got a good answer. It is not what I expect of you, but what you expect of you. And that is what I expected of you.

Now before I bid you a fond good evening let me tell you that those of you who come to class regularly and gravitate here, if you have not already discovered this for yourself, are the black sheep of the universe. You want to go your own way. You do not want dogma. You will not be satisfied with hearts and flowers. It is not an easy way, and all of you know that. It is past the time for you to be entranced by other personalities including my own. It is time for you to become entranced with your own personality. It is time for you to feel independent enough to launch yourselves from your own subjective reality into others; to emerge, to drop the paraphernalia of all dogma. Not for new dogma but for new freedom. Not to substitute one authority for another, but to allow yourselves the freedom to recognize that the prime authority is All That Is that resides within you and that speaks with your own voice.

(To Mary Ellen.) Listen to your own voice, proudly and gladly. Do not feel you need to go to others but acknowledge the authority that resides within yourselves and in that way you develop and use your own abilities.

(To Mark.) And you over there, become more loose in your experiments. You have the determination that this one has *(Gert)*, but you need the looseness, and it will come easily if you allow it to.

Now this is a big occasion for our friend, Ruburt, since his writing desk and all his materials are now in the other room. And as I always do to show not only guests and seeming strangers the nature of vitality but always to impress it as deeply as possible into your knowledge, then let me again remind you that this vitality is your own; that life, physical or nonphysical, is a full vitality that it is not necessarily quiet, that it is not necessarily sedate, and though my voice does not ring with the innocent chatter of children, that that same vitality that fills them fills me and fills each of you. That as you hear it here, feel it within yourselves. Let it rise. Life is not quiet, it is not sedate. All That Is is not some long-haired gentleman with a saintly face. And the soul that each of you believe in is not some quiet distant note far divorced from your own reality. It is a pulse that beats within you and the pupil of your eye and the big toe of your foot and your elbow. It is not necessarily adult. It is not necessarily dignified. It is the force that gives you all life and do not restrain it.

And so I bid you all a fond good evening, even to our Chinese friend over here. And those blessings that I have to give I give you, and those I have not you will have to search for.

ESP CLASS SESSION, JUNE 22, 1971 TUESDAY

(Following a discussion of everyone's experiences during the week.) Now I want you to get used to Alpha II and so I would like you to take your eyes off this charming face and close your eyes. Now I want you to realize that your perceptions at this point are limited only because you have previously chosen to limit them. The inner senses, however, are free. Your perception is not ideally limited and it is not practically limited once you realize this. In Alpha I you are used to one short adjacent step away from what you call your consciousness.

Now I want you to take one other step beyond this. I want you to realize that you are indeed highly perceptive, that around you and about you in all directions the inner senses reach. That you are in the midst of other realities. You are in the habit of blocking out, and you are now learning to accept them; to open up your perceptions; to open doors that have been closed.

Therefore, I want you to imagine in your mind

Alpha II and a door that has been closed and that now opens. It is an adjacent door. It is a place where you have walked often. You may see different signs and pictures in your mind, individually, as you open this door, for there will be different meanings here for each of you. But I want you to see yourselves opening that door and walking through.

Beyond that door are realities of which you have always known and people with whom you have always been acquainted. I want you to freely open the inner eyes and see their faces. Open the inner core and hear their voices. I want you to walk freely and with joy within these other realities that exist now as surely as this room exists.

I want you, therefore, one by one, to open the inner senses and to direct them along these lines. The physical body will not hinder you. In fact it will help you, for even hidden within the flesh are mechanisms that *[will]* help the inner senses *[to]* operate even in this environment. And so one by one, the inner senses can begin to operate so that what you see can become clear, and what you hear can become vocal and clear and strong. I want you to realize that you are getting glimpses of a reality that exists now, in your terms, that existed in the past and, in your terms, it will exist in the future. And a reality that is nevertheless instantaneous and as a part of you as your own heartbeat. I want you to learn to manipulate in that environment. I want you freely within it to look about. I want you to recognize the core of identity within yourselves that is familiar with this inner environment, for from your viewpoint other realities also open. Other doors that you can also enter; other channels into knowledge that are yours for the asking. I want you to rest now here for a moment. *(Long pause.)*

Now I want you to continue onward and in your mind visualize, if you prefer, still another door or a path or an avenue, or an alley, or a street, or a landscape; but still another reality that opens adjacently from this one. A reality that is involved with probabilities; and, as you glimpse that reality, you see that it is far vaster, and that it opens up into still other areas and fields and rooms.

From this viewpoint you can sense the other probabilities that reach outward from yourself like rays of light. The other probabilities that you have brought into existence and creation and song automatically, joyfully and creatively. I want you to feel their reality, their strength and vitality and to realize that they also reinforce your own life and your own existence.

Now I want those of you who can to follow still further, for we will travel beyond these fields of probabilities in which all times are born. Into another dimension in which times are not manufactured and moments of any kind do not exist. Into an immense system of beginnings that are beyond any beginnings that you may have imagined, in which all nebulous creations exist in incipient form. In which all probabilities exist, in your terms, as yet unborn; and yet in greater terms already being accomplished and coming into new existence. And you also have a reality here; and this reality, to some extent, nurses your own existence and reaches down into the system that you know, even though you are usually not acquainted with this reality. And this is only at the edges and the boundaries of the one system in which you have your existence. For beyond this, there are still other beginnings so alien that I cannot explain them, and yet they are connected with your own life; and they find existence and expression even in the small cells within your physical flesh.

And now I am going to ask you to return slowly back through these dimensions, pausing but briefly. I am going to try to put physical existence into a different perspective for you. You are all born into this time and this place.

Someone here this evening mentioned that it seemed that you only learn what life is and who you are and then your life is over; the time is brief. Another student mentioned an elderly father. Those of you who have parents living see them daily grow older, and the scorn of youth turns to the compassion that comes with years, and the bravado changes to understanding. And yet, within the understanding there is also bravado.

You are teaching yourselves the value of consciousness and vitality and strength and life, by pretending to yourselves that death is death and that your consciousness will not continue and that your parents who die are forever still, by pretending that the voices you have heard in childhood will be heard no more. By pretending that when you breathe your last breath here, your consciousness is forever still. You are teaching yourselves the value of being, and you have chosen this context in which to do it. You have chosen for the unoperable intimacy of tragedy and flesh and pain in order to teach yourselves the unoperable exultant nature of your own vitality and energy and song. And these lessons serve you well, and what you learn goes out from you in all directions and each triumph that you make is not yours alone, but reaches even into those dimensions of which I have spoken.

Now I ask you to return fondly to your image and the knowledge of it. To the intimate knowledge of flesh and bone and cell. To the intimate knowledge of the earth from which now, at least, you spring and to which the seed seems to return, for you have chosen a good teacher, the earth that you have created. Therefore, trust it and open your eyes and return your attention to the room.

(During break a discussion of each one's experience in Alpha.)

I am not finished with you. We are going to get into more of an emotional level also, in later classes. I will not let you forget that, you see, but for tonight the experiment is not over.

(To Buddy:) The answers are within yourself. Trust yourself. Do not go running from teacher to teacher. All they know, teachers, is how to look inward. Look inward into your own reality, and find your own freedoms, your

SESSION 6/22/1971

own truths, your own way, your own questions and these will lead to your own answers.

Now I want you to do several things. First of all, through listening to my voice, I want you to be reminded of the sheer physical vitality that is now a part of your own being. The physical life that you do not understand, that is now the vehicle for the expression of your self. I want you to be intimately aware of it and realize that the blood rushes within your veins with as much force as this voice speaks. Then I want you to give us a brief moment while I show you, to some extent, the vast distances, in your terms, in which your reality has its meaning. The dimensions of existence in which you also have your part.

(Long pause and Jane goes into a deeper trance.)

(Seth II:) Certain translations are being made for you so that these communications make sense to you. We would like you to close your eyes or unfocus them. Your thoughts suggest that you use these sounds and guidelines. Those among you who can follow, then hold onto these sounds and let them carry you with our trying an experiment at your Seth's suggestion. Our energy is as vital, far more than you own. Our energy forms worlds. The excess of our energy spills over into other creations. We help maintain your lives as you help maintain existences of which you have no knowledge. We watch you as you watch others, yet so vast is the distance, in your terms, that communication is difficult. We do not watch as human forms. You perceive us that way in a distorted view. In your terms, our forms would be geometrical. We

do not understand too clearly the nature of the reality that you are creating even though the seeds were given to you by us. We respect it and revere it. We watch it as we watch others. Do not let the weak sounds that reach you confuse you. The strength behind them would form the world as you know it and sustain it for centuries.

(During break there was a discussion of the above.)

(Seth:) I do indeed bid you all a fond good evening and the experiment continues and it will continue for the week while you go about your daily chores. Now there is nothing to prevent you from watching the watchers, you know, and this should intrigue you, and you particularly.

([Ron L.:] "Do you see, in other words, when Jane is speaking can you see the room or do you only see the room?...")

When I am speaking—when I am speaking I force myself to concentrate upon this minute portion of space and time that you think of as this room at this time. When Ruburt is Ruburt, or if you prefer, when Ruburt is Jane, then I let him take care of his own perceptions and I am simply aware of you as you are. That means I am aware of your identities as they are, and I am not limited by the one person you think you are at this time. So I can look at you, for example, knowing your reincarnational existences, and I am not limited to communicating to the one self you think yourself to be.

([Ron:] "Would you be aware of, say the pot on the table?")

Only if I were interested in the pot on the table.

([Ron:] "How would it appear to you?")

As a pot on the table.

([Ron:] "The same way it would appear...?")

When I use perceptions in your reality then I automatically translate inner data into physical terms, otherwise I am not limited to that kind of perception. I can view what you think of as that pot in many different ways for example. I need not perceive it as a pot but I can perceive it as a pot. You must perceive it as a pot.

And now I am saying good evening...

([Ron:] "You didn't answer my question.")

I did, indeed, you did not listen to the answer. Your questions obsessed you and you do not listen.

(Ron:] "It was just a general question of, could you see the room in the same terms that we see it, when you're not looking through Jane's eyes, if you wanted to or would it...")

If I wanted to, indeed, but there would be little reason to so limit my own perception of it. Its reality as you know it is a portion of my entire perception of it. Now, when you get the session the entire answer, as simply as possible, is given in that last sentence.

([Ron:] "You answered the question, I understand.")

Thank you.

([Buddy:] "What is your destiny?")

I do not know my destiny even any more than a raindrop does. I trust the nature of vitality and being and because I am I fulfill my destiny as you fulfill your own destiny simply through being.

([Buddy:] "And that is the answer to it all?")

That is the answer to the question that you have

asked me as you asked it. It is not the answer to the nature of reality or to the responsibility of consciousness.

([Buddy:] "Then can we talk about that sometime?")

We can indeed.

([Bette:] "Last week you said that we are the black sheep of the universe and I want to know do all the black sheep of the universe have dimples?")

Now there are some matters that in the great profundity of my nature even I do not have an answer to, and that is a question that we will have to refer to greater teachers than I.

([Natalie:] "Was there any truth to the impressions I received of resentment from Jane?")

There was such a relationship, and our friend took very sadly to a menial position for it followed one in which he was a great leader. And in the second one he tried to teach himself humility. And he was a slower learner indeed.

And now I do bid you a fond good evening, remembering that the experiment continues.

ESP CLASS SESSION, JUNE 29, 1971
TUESDAY

(Following a discussion of last week's class.)

(Seth II:) The experiment continues. I ask those of you who are ready to follow with me as we have observed

you then in your own way as you are able follow us. We are trying to not observe, as much as appreciate, the nature of your present existence; so those of you who are curious and willing about the nature of nonphysical reality then follow as far as you can, using the voice as a guideline into existence that has no reality in physical terms, that knows neither blood nor tissue, that knows not hand or finger or arm. Follow then beyond the knowledge of the flesh to those domains from which flesh was born and is born. Feel the kernel of your consciousness rise as one of your seeds, higher beyond the knowledge of seasons, beyond the feeling of your days or moments, beyond the relationships of blood, beyond all those kinships which you take for granted. To you on the way there will be an unbearable loneliness. You are so used to relating to the warm victory of flesh it will seem isolated. There is no physical being with whom then you can relate; and yet, beyond this and through the isolation is a point of light that is consciousness, that pulses with the power behind all the emotions that you know and that feeds them, that sends them sparkling and tumbling down into the reality that you know. A warmth that forms the very pulse of physical existence and yet is born from the devotion of our isolation; that is born from the creativity that is beyond flesh and bone, that forms fingers without feeling fingers, that forms seasons without knowing spring, that creates sand without knowing sand or ground, that creates the reality that you know without experiencing it, that forms fathers, sons and daughters and mothers without knowing what fathers and mothers and daughters and sons are, and yet from this devotion, from that creativity comes all that you know. And all of that also has been given to us for the energy that we have is not ours alone, nor are we the source of it; for it flows through us as it flows through you. The experiment then continues as it has continued, but you were not aware of it.

(Following a discussion of the above.)

(Seth:) Now I am not open to questions this evening. That will take care of that.

(To Joel.) I want to make a remark to you. Your image was an excellent one and in your terms it represents the characteristics of space as you might relate to it and also to those black pockets of which the physicists are speaking where all realities swooped into these, so to speak. But these are other dimensions of actuality where the reality that you know automatically is translated in different terms not, however, annihilated there as it seems, but translated.

Now earlier Ruburt told you to take two steps to the left. Now you are ready for a further development in your abilities and two steps at that image will help you for there is a highly dependable personality, and we will not argue over the terms, in approximately that area that, in your terms is a composite of Bill and someone else. A growth of Bill, if you prefer, and that can be your personal key to contact.

Now you have all been experiencing, the regular

student*[s]* to some degree, mobility of consciousness. You are learning to use the inner self as you learn to use arms and legs. And as we continue you will find yourselves in other levels of reality and able to manipulate within them. This is merely a beginning of courses in which you will become involved and you will meet your selves in those other levels of actuality as on several occasions you seem to meet yourselves in reincarnational situations in this room, so that you will be able to relate not only to the physical individual in this space and in this time and in this room, but also able to relate to other portions of your personality, in your terms, that existed in the past or will exist in the future. And understand you have done very little work along the lines of your future in those terms.

Now I am doing this to help Ruburt all the way down and also to give you some information for that symbol was a good one *(to Joel)*.

To those of you who are not regular students I bid you welcome and both of you have hitchhiked through time also. It is harder to get rides that way.

([Joel:] "Bette and I have had this thing going tonight that carries back from other weeks about the Indian problem, but there are some powerful things here, and it sure would be nice if you wanted to talk about that a little bit.")

Why don't you play it through?

([Joel:] "Well, we almost did.")

Ruburt also spoke of reincarnational dreams.

([Joel:] "I kinda got the feeling this wouldn't be a good

night for it from Ruburt's point of view.")

I will take care of Ruburt. He is a good friend of mine. I will comment on whatever you get, but the time has also come for you to meet each other, not only as the people you know yourselves to be here, but as the people that you also know you have been and to admit those recognitions that are beginning to flash across your consciousness.

You are playing games now, acting in plays that you call present times and you take your roles very seriously, but there are other dramas going on at the same time. And our Lady of Florence will become involved in some of these. And let us see some of those acted out and released and the energy that is hidden there used constructively.

(To Valerie.) You are doing well, and I am glad to see a good smile from you for a change.

We are now having a Seth break.

I do bid you a fond good evening and I suggest that you pay particular attention not only to your dream periods but to your ordinary waking experience this week for clues as to your own reincarnational... *(words lost)*... and for clues also as to the nature of the experiment which is still continuing and whose nature you do not as yet completely understand. There should be an important class meeting at another level of reality and hopefully you will remember it. You will be asked questions. Examine the nature of the questions, and that is all that I will tell you.

And all those blessings that I have to give I do give

you and those that I do not have to give you will have to find for yourselves, but the ways are always there for you to find your own additional resources, each of you in your own way.

And now I do bid you a fond good evening even with your strange arms and legs as our friend... *(words lost)...*

ESP CLASS SESSION, JULY 6, 1971
TUESDAY

([Jane:] "I think if we leave our experiences at face value, we're not learning all we can. I think in that simple drama that went on between Bette and Joel, see, there's all kinds of answers that we haven't even begun to reach yet. And then to accept them at face value can lead us astray. A fantastic strength and energy in Bette over there, and in Joel. And to understand what they really did demands that we go beyond stereotyped conceptions. And that each demands on both of their parts great self-examination and understanding. To accept what each of you are trying to do in your own way.

"But I would think that Arnold as much as anyone else has been browbeaten by the stereotype. He wanted to speak for a personality like Joel speaks for a personality, or Jane does, or he wanted to get information in a given particular way. Where all the time he's got it, and he knows he's got it. But he just wanted it to come out in a particular way. Where all you have to do is say, you know, I don't give a goddamn how it comes

because you have it. Or where beneath your humility is a refusal to accept your own divinity."

([Arnold Pearson:] "I agree with your first statement."

([Jane:]) "Which is denial."

([Arnold:] "Which I don't agree."

([Jane:] " 'Cause you all have to come to terms with the divinity within yourselves, some with the demon aspect, but with the divinity. And if that's all you're afraid of, then there's nothing to fear.

"If I could just get, if I could just get any of you, you particularly, because you're brand new, I don't know you. You to try to experience the fantastic validity of this moment, or any moment in your life, in all its ramifications, and in all its dimensions, what a great thing that would be, and how much you'd have to tell other people. And if you could experience that purely and freely, despite anything I say, you know, on your own, completely, with all barriers down, how fantastic that would be for any of you, myself included, 'cause it's something that we all reach for. I'm getting conditioned now, I don't want to say, Sue, what are you getting? Sue, what are you getting?"

([Sue Watkins:] "Writer's cramp."

([Jane:] "Sue's taking notes."

([Student:] "I felt somewhat with what we're doing in class ...I'm getting a bunch of writing ...."

([Jane:] "Great. I feel we have a tremendous amount of strength and energy, and we can really use it now; much more than we could have before. But if you're waiting for me to have Seth come through, you should be as anxious to hear your own inner selves come through. And if I show to you

various quite different aspects of personality, then you should feel them in yourselves, because they're all yours. You're just so used to concentrating on this one part of you that you insist is yourself, that you are not able to make these shifts. Now I can make them. I'm learning to make them more and more. But you can also make them without any sense of division, with a sense of complete easiness, and that's what I want you to learn to do. And I have taken away some of your comfort blankets, but don't cry, 'cause I'll give you something better instead."

([Bette Zahorian:] "And I just sat here for five minutes telling you to put that goddamn pen down, that he's been banging away, and he finally did it."

([Student:] "Why didn't you just tell me?"

([Bette:] "If you kept it up, I was just going to forget the thought and then get up and grab it."

([Jane:] "The thing of it is see, you look for wonders from me when you should look for wonders from yourselves. And there are wonders. You think there aren't any. There's all kinds of wonders from yourselves. Each one of you...fantastic. And with this thing I wrote tonight, I also got the idea that since we're being personally addressed if we listen, that to some degree the messages will be different. They will be addressed to us individually, knowing our needs and our characteristics, and all this stuff, so you will get the message ...different. Anyhow, that's okay.

"But I know, if I looked at each of you and the selves you think you are, with just the little experience I've got of the self I thought I was and find I'm not, that you have all kinds of

potentialities right now, not that you necessarily have to wait for or work for or anything, but that you have now. And when you look at me and want Seth to come through, and when you don't want to know what Jane says but you want to know what Seth says, you are denying your own reality. You are denying your own inner voice. Because you're saying, well, Jane is just an individual, and she can't know but Seth knows, and I'm an individual and I don't know, but Seth knows. But without me Seth couldn't speak, and without your inner selves you wouldn't have the knowledge.

"I saw last week as Bill started to speak, the class swerved, and everybody looked and listened to the new teacher, hoping that he would have the new answers; that if you couched your questions differently he would give you the answers. That somebody would say, here the answers are, this is it. Joel has seen this as people would shift from his group to my group. I've seen it as Buddy would come from here to the other guy. Where people run to others always, and where the messages we give, look within. You listen and it sounds great, but you ignore it to some extent or another. I shouldn't say this here because most of you to some extent or another, and some of you to a very great extent, are looking in and are doing this. But the divinity, and there is divinity, is within you, as well as within me, as well as within a tree, and that's what I want to teach you. And that's why class <u>will</u> continue."

([Bette:] "I want to say one little thing. When Bill came through, certainly we all looked. It was somebody that some of us here, I hadn't heard before. I talked to him because he talked to me. If he hadn't, I wouldn't have pushed in to talk to

Bill. I enjoyed talking with him. But as far as thinking that I could learn any more by listening to him than I could from coming here, or just listening to myself because if Joel is capable of doing this, so am I. If he can look in, so can I."

([Jane:] "Okay."

([Student:] "That's good, but what you're saying [referring to Jane] is true too, because looking back on it, it was exactly the feeling I had when I... Joel looked at me, I thought, maybe something will happen."

([Jane:] "It was sort of sad because I thought as I watched you all gravitate, I thought, they look at me as uncritically."

([Bette:] "I don't think that's fair to say that we all did that Jane. I didn't. I looked. Certainly I looked."

([Jane:] "And I don't want Joel to let himself be set up either."

([Joel:] "The reason that Bill didn't come through a long time ago was precisely as Jane says, and I don't care what anybody says anymore."

([Jane:] "Joel feels that need, see."

([Bette to Jane:] "But you have said in class to Joel, anytime that he feels he wants to let Bill come through, by all means do it. Am I right?"

([Jane:] "Yea, Bette."

([Student:] "I just wanted to be heard before we got off the subject. The class dream I couldn't remember was precisely just what you [Jane] were saying right now, and I did mention something this evening before class started that I just remembered. Seth was speaking. He wanted to know why,

just what you said, we all gravitate in that particular area; why we just heard one voice over another, or did we or should we and so on; just exactly what you said …I told you before class started."

([Jane:] "All I want you to do is if you hear your own voice, not to distrust it. I mean, why because it's somebody else's voice does it all of a sudden attain authenticity, where your own voice doesn't? You distrust your own experience and for some odd reason trust other people's, and this is what I want you to get away from."

(Class discussion.)

Now I have never said I was a nondescript personality floating through space. Not only would I not say it of me, I would not say it of you, and I would not like it, and I do not like it when you say it of yourself. You are each unique and individual and you are each highly original and as Ruburt has so nicely said, you each have your own paths into experience and understanding.

([Joel:] "A substitute instead of nondescript—what I was trying to say was rigidly defined. I can't accept that we are rigidly defined and structured as personalities.")

You are correct. I will tell you what I have tried to tell you a million times in my own way, and what I try to show you through those aspects of my personality that come through to you, and what in my teachings differs from any others, and it is this. There is joy and vitality in your physical existence.

Now, I hope when this is recorded you will read these statements simply several times for I am saying this

SESSION 7/6/1971

as clearly as I can. These are the ways in which what I say differs from those stereotyped stories of which Ruburt was speaking. First of all, there is nothing wrong with physical existence. You are not born through any sin, either original sin or Freudian sin. You are not either the products of some experiment that did not work on the part of superior scientists from another planet. You are not automatically hampered with. You are not automatically flawed. There is nothing automatically wrong with you. There is a spirituality within your tissues.

Physical existence is sacred and good. There is nothing wrong with it. Atoms and molecules, they are holy. Your consciousness is holy and so is your little toe. You can aspire. You must aspire for that is within you. But All That Is is now within you. You do not have to traverse worlds, you do not have to meet hopeless little gods at doorways to let you know whether or not you can enter or follow through on tests as some psychics tell you. You do not have to take upon yourselves definite <u>rituals</u>. You have only to look within yourself for the source of exaltation, creativity and song.

Now Ruburt has often wondered about this voice and so have you, and how I use it, and the sounds automatically, as they grow louder, increase the acceleration of your consciousness. They change vibrations of which you are not aware, they add, therefore, to the psychological bridge of which you are all part when you are in this room. There is no part of you that is not holy, that is not sacred, and that is not eternal. The answers are indeed within yourselves. They cannot be given to you by me. I can only show you the direction in which you must look, and the direction is within each of you.

Now Ruburt makes contact with me, but having made contact I am like some vital ever growing field that you finally reach. It is up to you to wander in that field and pluck your own idiot flowers and find your own paths. Now at this moment the field is there. The field that is my reality and yet is your own reality, and you must intellectually probe it, and intuitively probe it, and find your own paths within it. Its sources rise from your own being and from the fountainhead of creativity that is within each of you, and the teacher is within each of you, and you are yourselves the teacher that you do not recognize. And the voice that speaks in your dreams is the voice of yourself that you do not recognize speaking from the ancient founts of knowledge that are your own. I have told you often that I am no spooky guide that speaks in the night. I am myself, but I am also the speechless portion of your own selves. I am heights that you have reached and do not know that you have reached. I am your own heartbeat. I do have my own individuality yet this in no way means that there is not a meeting ground between what I am and what you are.

I have told you, the regular students, that you are finished with kindergarten. You have been telling secrets on another level in reincarnational terms. It is an extension of what you were doing earlier, an acceleration. I want you to look through the images that are not there that you see in your minds. I want you to look through the gods and the devils to see beyond these. I want you to look through the victim and the slayer. I want you to look through stereotyped images of good and evil until you understand what your own creativity is.

I want you to understand that in this moment in your time, your very cells respond to what I say, not because I say it, but because your cells also speak through my voice and the forgotten portions of you to which you do not listen. The voice that cries in the wilderness is your own, and the voice that answers from eons of time, that you do not understand, is your own. You have counterparts, you are not alone. You have brothers and sisters that you do not recognize.

Stratums that fly through the night, in your terms now, have known consciousness and song. The air that brushes past your cheek is alive. It too has known love and exaltation and will again. In what I am saying there are answers for you if you have the wits to catch on. In the power that you sense there are answers if you have the wits to sense within yourself that same power. To feel within the timbres of the voice the ecstasy that sings through your own being. To listen to all the tales that your selves tell you, to the secrets that fly through the air, and that is what I have been telling you all this time.

(During break Astor gave his views of Seth and the material.)

(To Astor.) Now you have heard me before and listened to me before, and you have argued with me as this

one over here now loves to do. And there was a time when you and Ruburt played in the rivers together as children. I did indeed say to this group it was a fairly good approximation of my manner.

Now I provide you with a bridge, and I have told you this before. You experience me as a particular personality, and you relate to it, and I, in turn, relate to you as the particular personalities that you think you are. That does not mean that what you see of my personality defines me, or that what you think of as your own personality defines you.

(To Joel and Bette.) You escaped from your current physical roles in class last week, our cousin of Richelieu, and our friend who loves the idiot flower, you experienced your emotional reality on an entirely different level. You encountered your own meaning and in different context.

There are other meanings and other contexts. Do not, therefore, think of that reality as the only one, for in other contexts there were changes of roles between both slayer and victim. Remember that.

And now because our cousin of Richelieu over here felt so sad and so despondent, I will leave you with that energy that is, after all, inherently your own. It will even confound our friend who yawns over here.

Remember, therefore, that your own vitality is without bounds. That it is ever new. That it sweeps through your own frame as easily and as naturally as the energy sweeps through this form. That you have only to accept

SESSION 7/6/1971

it and acknowledge it, and again that the vitality of life is not quiet; it is not adult; it is not dignified; it is. All the alleyways down which you have traveled have openings. Any disasters that you have worked upon yourselves have openings. Any energy that you need to direct to any part of your physical image is yours for the asking. Any thought that you have is creative.

When you listen, do not only listen but feel and within the energy of this voice feel, therefore, the energy within yourselves, within your spirits and your tissues, for you are now presently dwelling within tissue which you have also formed. Know, therefore, your own exaltation and your own energy and your own strength. Feel within yourselves that confidence and power and draw upon it as you go about your daily way. And feel it within you for it comes easily. As easily and miraculously as a flower grows, or as a hair grows out of your skull, or as a thought rises from your brain, that energy resides within you. That energy is your own—your own divinity rests within it. The bridgeways that you form, and that all of you know are made of this vitality. In silence it grows and is nurtured, but it is not of itself quiet. It is vigorous, and it is not afraid of quiet. It forms you. Get on good terms with it and do not deny it.

Now I bid you all a fond good evening, and yet before I do, I ask you to identify with the power behind this voice and to feel it within your very cells, for it is your own power, your own energy, your own knowledge and the divinity from which you have sprung and which is a part of each of you. The voice that answers is your own, then listen to it with love and understanding.

Those blessings which are mine I give you *(pause)*.

([Joel:] "And those you don't have we'll have to find ourselves, and when we find them ourselves you can give them to us.")

Now that is what I have been waiting for you to discover. Peace.

ESP CLASS SESSION, JULY 13, 1971
TUESDAY

(Following a discussion on reincarnation.)

Now you are both channels, in those terms, for what you might think of as both white holes and black holes. You are channels through which various realities merge and meet and in which transmutations constantly occur. You are yourselves, then, warps in the universe as you think of it. You are meeting places where other realities merge and meet. You are intersections, cosmic intersections, and it is up to you as the conscious selves that you think you are now, to listen and watch and to be aware of these portions of your personality that flow through you and in and out of you, in your terms.

(To Bette and Joel.) In other words, your experience and your experience as encountered in class in a reincarnational framework did indeed, and does indeed, and will indeed, in certain terms exist.

And the time has come for you to experience fresh and new concepts and to find them within yourselves for the miracle of consciousness is your own as it is my own, or Ruburt's own. You are each the miracles of consciousness, and those miracles occur within you constantly in your terms of time. Therefore, each of you possess within yourselves inroads, or if you prefer outroads, where other portions of reality and other selves merge and reemerge, come and go, materialize, in your terms, and dematerialize. The answers, as you know therefore, are not only within yourself but pass through you automatically if you but realize it and know it. And within yourselves you each possess in miniature all the properties of the universe as you conceive of it at this present time.

So what it seems to you or to your scientists occurs outside of you, occurs within you, and now. Not theoretically, not merely in intuitive terms, but altogether at once regardless of the concepts that you attach to the experience. This is what I hope not to teach you, but to lead you to understand and experience for yourselves. To understand that you are each at the meeting points of the universe and of experience. And that what you observe does not necessarily come from outside of you but from inside of you. I hope to give you the confidence to grasp the freedom then to explore yourselves, easily, freely and joyfully as one of our friends, the flowers, might suddenly choose to explore itself in all its uniqueness.

([Joel:] "In one of the stories that Jane wrote, the guy went down to the beach with the wind chimes and (words lost)

tree and he selected atoms and that somehow absorbed them through himself into another system until there wasn't any physical world that we know of left at all, and then as I recall at the end he popped through his whole universe and isn't that somewhat the same kind of thing? He was the black hole for awhile then he ran around the other side of the set and became the white hole and the whole transfer occurred through him and the whole thing may have been a symbol and that this occurs back and forth and constantly in all of us all the time.")

It does, indeed, and you peek in and out of yourselves in line with what I have said earlier about the pulsations.

([Arnold:] "There isn't really any outside to us is there? So everything is within us.")

There is not, indeed, the outside is within you, and anything you think you see outside originates within.

([Tom D:] "...could not hear the questions.")

You always create it. You create and form your own reality, but you create and form more realities than you consciously realize. Now it is possible, you see, and you are trying to bring what you think of as your conscious self into some awareness of what these other portions of the inner self are up to so, supposing we call your presently conscious self your immediate self. Will you accept that phrase? All right. So we will say you all have immediate selves which deal with the here and now, in those terms. Now the immediate self can indeed become aware of other portions of your own reality, and it is up to you to bring it into line. To some extent you can do this, not entirely, but intuitively you can make great strides. You may not be able to translate the experience clearly, but you may be able to translate it capably enough so that you realize, so that the immediate self realizes, that it is indeed a part of other experiences.

(To Bette.) You are doing this to some extent with your reincarnational dramas, and when you do this you see you are bringing others up to date, in those terms, also.

(Tom D. spoke of his ability to teach the lower classes easier than to teach the average middle-class children.)

Now All That Is is as much in middle class America as it is in India. All That Is resides as much in the poor suburbanite who mows his lawn and has his endless mortgage as it does in a guru who sits upon his mat. The anguish and the triumph is in each of you. And do not yourself fall into the stereotype of setting the establishment apart for it is also composed of exalted and anguished individuals.

([Tom D:] "What I was trying to say was, it is easier to influence the kids that are slow learners... less outside influence... It is easier to get to them than it is to get to the middle class who has got more stigmas... [inaudible].")

See yourself as a playful creator.

([Tom D:] "I feel that I am helping those kids.")

You are indeed. Playful creators always help. Creation is playful and full of joy but do not in your own heart set up any kind of social barrier. For when you do unknowingly, you do what has already been done to you and therefore perpetuate, to some extent, those stereotypes that so upset and annoy you. I understand your feeling and your sense of accomplishment but also remember in your heart that the most stereotyped unoriginal suburbanite, in your terms, has within him all the capabilities of which we speak so that you do not, in your own mind, set him down as a caste system for that is what has been done to you. Recognize in yourself the egos that you see in others.

(Remark by Tom D. was inaudible.)

I did not say you were evil and never would I say such a thing. When you read the record you will realize that is not what I said. I said, recognize within yourself those evils that you recognize in others, but I meant only those things that in your own mind you set up as evil for you project those things upon others and make your own reality. Now, the barriers you see do not exist in the children but in yourself. And that is what I want you to understand.

(Jane suggested we find our own symbol.)

To some extent Ruburt's voice was your own voice, the voice of each of you leading you on journeys that you wanted to take. Initiating adventures that you want yourselves to make.

(To Bette.) Our friend over here who insists on relating, not from the Richelieu experience but from another, did a very good job of realizing that the energy originates not from this form but from each of you. You need to put both of these reincarnational dramas to work. Read and

experienced together they will show you different portions of yourself. You find it much easier to relate to the one than to the other because to relate to the other you think would demand too much of you intellectually. And such is not the case.

([Ron Labadee:] "I wanted to throw something out. Several sessions ago we got into a conversation about the nature of the way you perceive this reality although we didn't get into your own particular...")

The ways in which I can perceive this reality.

([Ron:] "And you were saying that if you wanted that you could perceive it just as clearly in the same terms that we ourselves perceive it.")

In as limited terms.

([Ron:] "Well, what I was wondering is...")

The trouble with you is you have no sense of humor.

([Ron:] "Well, let's see how yours is. I would like to suggest an experiment and I am suggesting it to you to see your reaction, like I couldn't. I was really undecided whether to suggest it to Jane or to you, but you see like I'm kind of at an impasse because, like, there are a lot of words and a lot of concepts and philosophies bandied about, but when you make a claim you know such as that in as specific and non-confusable terms such as that it would be very simple to demonstrate, and what I was wondering is, either now or at some time when Jane would agree to it, for instance, I brought some playing cards with me, ten cards...")

Now my dear love. Jane may or may not look into

your playing cards. I do not know. That is up to her or to Ruburt. As far as I am concerned, I will not bother. Now we have been through this with keener minds than your own. The claims I make, I make not only for myself, but for you and for each person in this room. You can perceive those playing cards as clearly as I can, and if you will not believe me, you will not believe yourself. When I follow through with such demonstrations, I will do so not in the confines of this room and not under conditions set by you, but in a situation in which the claims are clearly recorded with the results in which there is no possibility that anyone will say suggestion is involved; in which no one will be able to say that scientific principles were not clearly set upon and not to satisfy your curiosity! You can, however, prove to yourself by reading the cards. I do not have the doubts, you do.

([Ron:] "Well you give me the impression though, I mean, like that's an easy way out.")

What is important are emotional realities not symbols upon cards and until you realize that and until you are willing to open up emotionally to the atmosphere of the class and to the room then no proofs will be proofs to you.

([Ron:] "Well, I would disagree very much with that. If you are able to do what you know even to a limited extent what you claim that you are able to do, I would be completely dumbfounded. However, I don't think...")

You are setting forth challenges in terms that you do not understand and until you understand that, that is the position at which you will remain.

([Ron:] "You could be equivocating.")

I could indeed and you can interpret what I am saying in any way that you choose. The fact remains that it is you, not I, who are worried about my perceptions. The fact remains that what we have done has been set clearly forth in the book that Ruburt has written. You can accept that, or you can deny it, and as far as Seth or Ruburt are concerned that is your right.

([Ron:] "We never read the results though.")

You are speaking about one specific group of tests and the doubt exists, you see, in your mind and while that particular kind of doubt exists nothing will convince you.

([Ron:] "To a certain extent, you know, you can always— you can bring my motivations into question, but I have like one overriding feeling and that is—I feel that within my own experience I have seen certain indications just from the things that I might be capable of that I could do this myself if, if when and if, because I have entertained the challenge of developing this ability but I in this situation here, I am confronted with kind of a different type of ramifications. What I am saying is, within this, within this context for me and for persons who would like to contribute to a communally verifiable and acceptable body of knowledge there are certain precise ways in which you could go about…")

And circus tricks are not part of those… are in your terms…?

([Ron:] "Yes, but would you consider Instream's experi-

ments a circus trick? And incidentally, the way he set up that experiment was atrocious for a man with scientific training.")

He was a delightful old gentleman, and he did the best that he could, and he does not need a whippersnapper like you to comment upon what he tried so hard to do. He could not accept the results.

([Ron:] "With my own training in psychology, I could set up a controlled airtight experiment. In other words, if you had made kind of a nebulous statement about the nature of your perceptivity, if you had said something...")

I am making statements about the nature of my perceptivity and your own. And you can accept the statements or not accept them, and that is entirely up to you.

([Ron:] "Obviously, no one can make decisions for me.")

And any work that is done, is done with Ruburt's consent, and our friend got his back up quite well after working for two years with psychologists. And if I were you, I would tiptoe out the door before someone tells him what you have come up with, for I am also dependent to some idea upon his receptivity and ideas. And that is exactly as it should be.

([Ron:] "Yes, exactly which is why I said it would have to be something, it could be something that could be arranged.")

He is not any more interested than I am now in such experiments.

([Ron:] "Why aren't you interested?")

At one time he was highly interested, and I went

along because it was a sort of proof that he found extremely necessary. When it was proven to him, I was satisfied. Whether it is proven, in those terms, to you or not bothers me not one iota. That is your thing. I was satisfied with the matter of his need for proof. When he attained it that took care of my end of it.

([Ron:] "Did he really attain it?")

He did, indeed. And your need in that particular line is your own. And peace in finding it.

([Ron:] "Yes it is my own, but...")

You see, you come with demands. Now those who have come open-mindedly to class have found their proofs; and proofs that were not dependent upon cards or showy tricks, but strong proof in that the nature of their reality changed. They understood themselves better. They would relate to the experience that they know. They had experiences that they did not have before, and their mental, psychological and spiritual worlds expanded. And to them, and to me, card reading is an entirely different and inferior product, but while that is what you are looking for you will find yourself at the level that you are now. Without strong subjective proof of your own, without the full ability to travel inward and the doorways to inner knowledge closed until you receive the kind of proof that you are after.

([Ron:] "So the answer in essence is that you yourself would not be interested in this because you don't consider it relevant even though...")

I do not consider it, at this time, revelant. I did

when Ruburt was so concerned.

([Ron:] "Even though for myself, you know, for my own personal point of view it would be something that would be very relevant and particularly in terms of the way I relate into this situation.")

([Arnold:] "It is relevant to no one of the rest of the class either. Nobody else in the class is interested in wasting time.")

([Ron:] "That's what I say—it could be something that—but I won't bring it up now because I wanted to hear your opinion of it.")

My opinion is that that I have given. Had you come here, however, when the sessions had shortly begun, and Ruburt was himself looking for that kind of proof, the answer may have been different. It is what I have given you now, however, and I fear that like our friend, Instream, unless you change you will be looking for proofs that mean nothing and ignoring the inner reality that is all important and closing your mind to inner validity that alone will give you the kind of proofs that you require. They will come from the inside and not from skepticism. And then you will see them. For example, had your attitude been different and your whole emotional atmosphere been different, and had you in a mood of fun and free giving thrown cards upon the table when I was speaking and said, "Seth, what is on the other side of the cards?" you may have gotten an answer. But not in the framework in which you asked the question nor in the framework in which you proposed the experiment.

([Ron:]) "Well, I don't know. I kind of doubt it, but as for looking inward, you know that there has to be a balance between the inwardness and outwardness."

([Sally:]) "Three years ago we went through all of this and it's in Jane's book."

([Gert:]) "Not only that, he didn't make himself part of the group, if you'll excuse me, and I hope we are not projecting again. When we let our Pandoras out of the box, you sat very placidly over here thinking, 'I'm going to keep mine in.' We gave and you demanded.")

Now, before I let my friends very sweetly and nicely rush to my defense, let me mention that Ruburt also when classes began, made an effort, as our friend over here remembers, to give spontaneous readings which worked very well. This means that they checked out. He quickly found, however, that that was not the answer, that people merely said, "He has the answers, and I have none," that they projected upon him abilities that they thought they did not possess. And therefore he has changed that policy. Whenever evidential material has been given, my dear friend, and it has been given to help others deal with a problem that was of vital interest, it has not been given as a demonstration, and it has not been given to prove anything to anyone. And now I return you to our friend and we will switch channels.

And now I do say goodnight, and my heartiest regards to you and again those blessings that I have to give you, I give you and from the last session you know about those other blessings.

ESP CLASS SESSION, JULY 20, 1971
TUESDAY

(Joel mentioned he would like Seth's interpretation of his foliage image.)

With one word to our baiting friend over here. Now you are beginning to perceive what we will, for now, call biological realities in other spheres of reality. You are making transitions from the forms that you know, and the forms that you are used to perceiving, so that you can perceive other forms with which you presently are not acquainted. There will be, therefore, some distortion while your vision clears. You are looking through new windows.

Now I am glad that you have all had such a jolly evening, and in the table's energy I hope that you saw a reflection of your own *(to Ron)*, and I hope that you realize, not looking at anyone in particular, that a playful answer will be given and long faces will get you nowhere.

(To Daniel.) Now you must realize the vitality that is within each of you and not be afraid of it as you are. Now you are controlling it and disciplining it, but also, you are afraid of it. You simply bottled it up out of fear of your own ability and of the power that resides within you.

Now if you all want to play games some night, we will have some fun with the table. In the meantime, beneath the fun and games, feel your own vitality. Get to know it. Enjoy its sensation.

(To Sue.) Let it bring you, as it did you this week, to escape from ordinary ideas of time and limitations.

([Sue:] "Then the dream was valid?")

It was indeed to lift you, as it did you, in your dreams from the ordinary world that you know. Let it enable you to understand yourself better as you. Let it show you portions of your own identity as it has with our cousin of Richelieu *(to Bette)* and our secretary over here *(Natalie)*. Let it lead you into other aspects of consciousness and vitality as it is with our friend over here and to open doors of feeling as it has with you *(Alison Hess)*. Let it bring families closer together as it has in your case *(Janice)*. And let it above all, also arouse questions as it has with you *(Arnold)* and with you *(Tom D.)* but realize again that this vitality that rings through this voice rings through your own identity and yours. That the power beneath the voice is but a shadow of the vitality that is within each of you. Let it then give you confidence in your own identity and in your own reality. Move yourselves and tables will take care of themselves.

So those blessings that I have to give I give you, and you know the rest of that.

ESP CLASS SESSION, JULY 27, 1971
TUESDAY

(Edgar and Maria explained their method of healing by hypnosis. Edgar hypnotizes Maria and she, by scanning lights which she sees in the patient's chest, can read the symptoms. Edgar remarked he would like Seth's comments on their method.)

I bid you all a fond good evening, and I do indeed have something to say. I do want to comment on your experience and your work thus far. Now, I am a very fine, kind old gentleman, at least in this aspect, so you need not be nervous. I admit that the circumstances, the voice, may make me sound severe. This is a matter of the mechanics.

So you are embarked upon valuable work and experience. You are only beginning to ask the correct questions. Hypnosis is an excellent tool, you are using. It is valuable indeed. As you learn to ask the proper questions, it will become more valuable. You need to grow beyond the concern for the nature of the light. In the terms of which I am speaking, this is not the kind of question. That kind of question will only give you a certain kind of answer, and if you follow that course then you will follow a question-and-answer course, but without learning anything more than a series of questions and answers that have meaning only within a certain limited framework. So you must lead yourselves free of that.

Now I can tell you what the light is, but when I do

that, I am a poor teacher, for a good teacher knows how to let others discover meanings for themselves, and that is a part of your experience. Otherwise you would not be working with the light. The question is not, what is the nature of the light? That is one of the important things I wanted to tell you.

Now many in this class have been involved in many other sorts of a highly emotional nature, and so some of them are welded together in a certain way. There was a reason why there was no session last evening, and if you listen to the conversation, and if you understand the nature of suggestion as thoroughly as you should and must, then you will understand the reason.

(To Edgar) Now, and I say this with utmost kindness and good nature, you can tell Ruburt that you have no feelings, and you can tell the class that you have no feelings, and you can tell others that you do not care what is said or done to you, but do not tell me. Now in your position, you of all people, should recognize feelings within yourself, the effects of others upon you and be even more vigilant of the effect of what you say upon others.

(To Maria) And the same applies to you. Now you are deceptive, slyly, in your own manner, to yourself, for it seems to you that you are very aware of your emotions, and that they are clear and out in front of you, and that you are an emotional person, and yet you hide them deeply and the emotions that you show are not the emotions often that you feel. And they are guises to hide

other things that you do not face. This you should understand.

Now some of this has to do with some information given to you by Joseph last evening—Joseph is your friend Robert—having to do with your ideas of health and illness. You must learn to understand your motives and even with the hypnotic ability that your husband has, you still have not learned to understand your own motives using that tool. The fear of reincarnation is again a shield for another fear that you have not faced that has nothing to do with reincarnation but has charged the word reincarnation to you. The fear is not connected with reincarnation per se, but as long as you believe, unconsciously, that this is so, you will react in that manner. You can use the tool of hypnosis to a far greater degree than you are using it.

(To Edgar) And you must learn also to look beyond your own facade for you believe in it utterly, and yet it is not you. The work you are doing is valuable and can be, but it demands a high integrity of a kind you are only beginning to learn. By integrity, I am speaking of honesty with self that demands you to go beyond the self-deceptions that you accept as your self at any given point.

Now I bid you all welcome. I am sorry you are not moving tables for me this evening.

(To another student) You did indeed have some valid dream experiences, and you only remembered a portion of them. And as Ruburt told you earlier you were involved with a group before the time of Atlantis and you

have been together often. But many times you have been too exclusive in your relationship, again as Ruburt told you.

(To Edgar and Maria.) Now another thought. You must try to avoid an overconcentration now upon the negative simply because you are looking for symptoms with the people who come to you. This is extremely important, otherwise you can project also. Your own thoughts and feelings should be those of health and vitality so that these alone help in the healing process. Now these are things that you will learn, and I am not scolding you, do not look at me like that, or you will make me cry, but it is the only time I have to get a hold of you, and so I want you to understand what I am saying.

Now I will let you all take a break. You especially over there *(Sue)* and you *(Maria)* and you *(Joel)*, and you all know to what I am referring.

(To Maria.) You had your chance, you see, and you did not scan me.

(During break Edgar remarked Seth said he asked foolish questions. Several members of class remarked Edgar and Maria might be giving their patients negative suggestions. Maria remarked Seth yelled at her.)

I was not yelling at you. I explained the mechanics of the voice. It is not everyday I have young women cringing before me...

I am trying to show you I can smile. That is a smile... She's speechless. You see, I'm good for something.

(To Edgar) I did not say it was foolish to ask ques-

tions. Now when you read the text you will see that I simply said you were beginning to learn to ask the proper questions, for some questions can be traps that betray you.

(Jane gives reincarnational information to Edgar and Maria.)

There is something that you can do. There is something that all of you can do, and I have told the class this many times, but you tend to forget it. You can become far more aware of your own thoughts and feelings than you are now. Now you have much more knowledge available to you. As a rule you do not admit this knowledge. A truth about yourself will pop to the surface of your mind, and you will shove it down quickly rather than take advantage of it. I am not speaking now only to you *(Maria)*, but to everyone in the room, our friend, Ruburt, included.

You can become far more aware of your own thoughts and far more aware of your own honest attitudes. Often you do not approve of them, or they frighten you, and you shove them down into the other portions of your mind. There they can indeed do damage. If you get into the habit, however, of tuning into your own stream of consciousness you will find the person that sometimes will seem quite a stranger to you. And that person will be yourself. You will not only shove down ideas that seem negative, however, you will also shove down feelings of generosity, particularly toward people that you do not like, feelings of joy because you feel too guilty to think you should feel joy. You will shove down all kinds of impulses, and so you will not know yourself, and you will block off impulses that you really should accept, recognize and admit as portions of yourself.

(To Edgar) Now you should not sit back and say because a particular thing happened to me in the past I have this attitude. Once you realize that is the reason you must also know that you are an entire individual and can indeed change that pattern of reaction and feel within yourself that energy that you feel, that upsurge of strength and vitality that lets you know you can do this and court that feeling of energy and teach her to court it.

Ruburt will want to know if the door is closed, so tell him because I want our friend over here in the bridal white *(Maria)* to realize that each of you should realize that the energy and strength and vitality that rings through this frail form now rings also through that form and that form and that form and represents the energy and vitality that belongs to each of you, and you all have it to draw upon.

(Maria had scanned Jane the previous evening. While Seth was speaking Edgar hypnotized Maria so she could scan Seth and wondered if Maria should tell Seth or Jane her findings.)

You will tell Ruburt. First let some energy flow through your own being and feel it refresh you and make you young and strong and vital and know that it resides within you all of the time. That you can rely upon it easily and with confidence, that it is yours for the asking, that it resides within you. That it is your right and your heritage.

(To Edgar) As it is your right and your heritage.

(Edgar brought Maria out of trance. Maria remarked there was no change or fluctuation in the lights while Seth was speaking than she had seen in Jane the previous evening.)

Now Ruburt is not invaded when I speak. He is not taken over by another, his individuality is not violated in any way, and it is very important for you to realize that and to know it. It will give you confidence in your own work. You are dealing with an old wise experimenter right here, and you saw what you needed to see. Do not categorize your experience. In this instance you saw what you saw when you scanned. That is all you should make out of the situation. The individual is inviolate always.

([Joel:] "Was I right then about the aura changing because of the intensity of Jane's own mental focus?")

That effect is something else entirely and happens only on certain occasions, and it is caused by something quite different.

([Edgar:] "What is the attraction between us two [meaning to Sue]?")

You must work that out for yourselves. That is an important part of the class framework, and if you are ready to work it out for yourselves you do so. If you are not ready, I will not tell you. This also has to do with other feelings on your parts here *(Sue)* and here *(Maria)*, to some extent over there *(Joel)*. And as you all know in this room when you feel ready to accept new experience and work it through, you will do so.

Now I bid you good evening rather late in the game and the same to you. And those blessings I have to give I give you, and you know where you will have to find the rest.

(To Daniel) And you will make out all right. Do not worry about tables chasing you about the room.

(To Arnold.) Your dream was valid. You were correct about your dream. You have no idea.

([Joel:] "Who were you pointing to when you said that somebody over here had something else to work out. We are not sure.")

I was speaking about feelings directed toward our friend here *(Edgar)* and I was pointing at you. I was pointing at you and at you *(Sue)* and at you *(Maria).* There were others, also, but the feelings in this case were of a different nature. The same applies to Ruburt and the both of you.

(Seth returned.) If you are ready to tell secrets we're all ready to listen. I've said good night before you asked the question.

(Class discussion.)

(To Maria.) Because you have not read my book. I bid you all good evening.

You are in a trance state now, and you have all hypnotized yourselves into believing that this is the only reality and your constant suggestions continue the emotion, and that is the basis of your physical reality. And I did mean to interrupt you. That shows you I am gracious.

(To Daniel.) And for our friend over here, and not really for him but for our long-faced friend who is not present tonight *(meaning Ron)*, Ruburt will go for any tests that are fun. That means any tests that he likes the idea of, so you can pass the word along.

ESP CLASS SESSION, AUGUST 3, 1971 TUESDAY

(Following a discussion of everyone's experience for the week and a mobility of consciousness exercise.)

I welcome those who are new this evening, but I have some remarks for our regular students having to do with your dreams. We mentioned sometime ago an experiment. Now the visitors that have been here until this evening had a part to play in that experiment. Other portions of the experiment, however, are concerned with your dream states and those individuals that you are meeting. Besides the associates and friends that you know in your daily waking life, you also have a quite legitimate relationship with people that you do not know as you go about your daily concerns. And you perform work of which you are unaware as you go about your daily way.

Now some of you are ready to meet these other associates. They are people living on the face of the earth at this time. People that you have never met physically and probably will never meet, in those terms, but you are involved often as apprentices in joint endeavors and it is time that you become aware to some extent of your relationship. Those that escape you in the dream state. Therefore, I want you to take particular notice of people in your dreams who are strangers to you. You may encounter them in class dreams. You may also encounter them, however, in dreams that seem to have no great meaning. These people cooperate with you as you cooperate with them. You are involved with many activities. Helping people who have died, in your terms, speaking to others who are quite alive, in the dream state, learning to understand and manipulate subjective realities.

Now there are two main possibilities that can emerge here, and these people can become quite real to you. You have begun to become aware of some of your own reincarnational existences. Because of this you have been able to relate to yourself and to others in a more effective manner and to understand others from a different point of view. Now, however, you should also become aware of other personalities who work with you when your normally conscious ego is quieted. Some of you already have clues.

Now this requires some study and means that you will have to remember your dreams much more effectively than some of you are doing. And I am giving you the impetus. When possible think of these persons also when you discover them so that in your daily waking life you can receive some more intuitional information as to the kind of work and endeavors in which you are all involved. We want you to become aware of all of your activities, not simply your conscious ones. You are using abilities in that work that you are not using as yet in your conscious lives, and I want you to become aware of what these abilities are. They can also help you deal much more effectively with physical reality and help you understand it far better. You may find several of you involved in the same work in the dream state. And so, also, keep track of whatever class members may appear within these dreams. Then when you are doing well in class, you will be able to relate not only to some reincarnational selves but to the inner self and to its activities and use these activities to enrich your normal daily encounters and to increase the nature and extent of your perceptions.

Now we are having a Seth break and not a class break.

([Joel:] "You said 'we want you' to be aware etc. Would you expand on the we a little bit?")

Not at this time. I will, however, later.

([Joel:] "After we think about it awhile?")

Indeed. I notice it did not miss your attention, however.

([Gert:] "Would we at anytime hallucinate, say, the strangers?")

You hallucinate the reality that you know to begin with.

([Gert:] "In the dream state, these strangers or associates, would we put on them a face that we would be able to relate to, say, a member of our family?")

These will appear to you as strangers and not as

SESSION 8/3/1971

people that you know.

([Gert:] "Would you help me with one thing, please? I have been trying to workout something with my oldest daughter. I don't know what, but I feel there is something there that should be worked out, so I gave myself the suggestion for a dream concerning this, and I got one which dealt with my older brother Tommy. In it I was telling him to sit down, and I was trying to talk to him, but I couldn't, but finally I did and what I'm wondering, because I've had this three or four times in the dream state, trying to talk. The other times it has happened it scared me, and I tried to call my husband.")

Now, do you want the information now?

([Gert:] "Yes."

In the back of your mind you have wanted the girl to be a boy. You go out of your way permitting her to behave in what you think of as a feminine fashion. But in the back of your mind you still think that the male holds the position of leadership, and therefore, you resent your own feelings when you try to have the girl behave in that feminine manner. You are trying to order her to be something—a female—when in your heart you wished she was a male, and so when you try to order her about in the dream instead you speak to the brother who is a male, and your words do not make a physical impression. You have difficulty. This is involved, therefore, with previous experience that you have discussed and simply means that you need more work along those lines to clear your own feelings. You are projecting them upon the child and into the relationship. I suggest, however, that you use your own means to probe into those feelings so that you work them out for yourself.

(During break Margie explained what they were studying in the Cayce class and what they want to attain. Bette asked Buddy if he was using the knowledge he had studied so long for.

(To Bette.) Now to our friend over here who should understand the reason for the question. Now if there is any discipline that I would tell you to adapt, it would be the discipline of joy which is spontaneous and from which, initially, all creativity comes. Within yourselves you understand the meaning of the word joy, then you will find no contradiction. Sorrow of itself can be negative or positive according to the reasons why you entertain it. Detachment can be negative or positive according to the reasons that you adapt it. Joy, faithfully followed, can lead you to the inner vitality that dwells within yourself and, hence, to All That Is.

If you understood and felt the joy within your own being, you would have no need of questions. You would know without words. If you would allow yourselves the freedom to meet, not some great teacher, not to run from teacher to teacher, but if you could meet the vitality within one cell, even one molecule of your body, you would have no need for questions.

(To Giovanni) Now I have a brief word that I would like to say to this one over here. Now first of all you are not afraid of psychic reality in any sense of the word. You are, however, worried about the nature of your own real-

ity and worried about how far you want to follow into the nature of your own feelings. You are intrigued, therefore, but held back. There is nothing wrong with that. It is a stage of becoming. Accept it and do not think necessarily that you must be otherwise, for if you go along with the feelings that you honestly have at any given time, they will become the feelings. If, however, you try to hide them from yourself, then they become like knots that bind you.

So admit to yourself both your fascination with the nature of reality, and your own search. And admit also those misgivings that you have and that rise to the surface of your mind for even those can lead you somewhere. Do not feel inferior because it seems to you that this one *(Nadine)* is going further or quicker or faster. You each will go your own way. And you can hold your own.

As so often happens you are each involved now, not only in this class, but with another. Now you need not close your eyes but if you listen to your own inner voice, and if you allow yourself the freedom, and if you understand the nature of probabilities, then as I speak and as you listen you can indeed, to some extent, perceive the other reality, the specific reality of which I am speaking in which you also exist as a group. And feel to some extent the gathering energy that unites you. The energy unites you here as it unites you there. The indirections of personality occur there as they do here but with some very important differences. There you can move tables easily and well. I would like you to allow yourselves the freedom of feeling that reality. It will add richness to the dimension of your own existence. I would like you to try to sense the similarities and the differences and particularly the differences in your own reaction to other students for there are some important ones. And in one of these classes you have been a member for some time *(Margie)*, so have you *(Wally)*. You have indeed.

Now some of the people also attending that class are the strangers that I spoke to you of, and that you know them well in the dream state. You are all so wise when you are sleeping. The abilities that you show are quite your own, and I would like to see you bring them to the surface and use them but then I am certain that you will do so. I cannot always speak to each of you individually, but I do speak to you individually and you should know what I mean by that sentence.

(To Ron L.) Now in another reality sometime you are really going to be put to the task of explaining to personalities who have no idea of the nature of physical existence, that physical existence does indeed exist. So you had better prepare yourselves with cards or otherwise. Those of you who are not members of the class, forgive us but that is an in joke.

(Sue explained to Jane we should become aware of a probable class.)

Now the members of your so-called probable class are involved, in your terms, at precisely this point with the same experiment. Therefore, of course, they consider this the probable class.

([Margie:] "Why this urgency to get to know this other probable system?")

Because they are yourselves. Because there is no division between you. Because it is a part of your own identity. Because you are learning then to become acquainted with the whole, or in your terms, to become acquainted with the entire reality of the soul as it has meaning to you.

([Margie:] "But there are many probable selves, are there not?")

There are indeed. Why should the soul be limited? The soul is not a thing that you have. The soul is not the consciousness that you know. The soul is far beyond the consciousness that you presently experience. It is only your own ideas of a limited self that make you think in terms of such a closed soul. There are no closed systems, and there is no end to the growth of the soul.

(Joel and Wally gave their interpretations of what Seth had said.)

I will bid you all a fond goodnight because our friend, Ruburt, is worried about the time. Also because I have said what I wanted to say, and I hope you heard our friends' interpretation for it was a good one *(Joel)* and this was a good one also *(Wally)*. I want you to stop identifying completely with the conscious self that you know, and I want you also to remember that I told you that though physically I may not speak to you individually in class, the messages are given, and I expect you to be expert enough to receive them. So if you feel left out it is only because you have not been aware enough.

No one can order you to feel joy. You cannot order yourselves to feel joy. It requires freedom. You can release yourselves to the sensation of joy and then follow it. I saw the yawn, and in the yawn there is joy. The yawn is a spontaneous expression of the body and within that there is joy.

I expect you to release your own energy both in the dream state and the waking state. I expect that each of you will become more and more aware of your own uniqueness. Be able to meet and recognize the realities of your own personality. To appreciate them as if you saw them suddenly appearing before you. To appreciate yourself as you might another. To be astonished and amazed with your own individuality.

(To Ron) I expect you to release those portions of your personality, and I am looking where you think I am looking. To release those portions freely and not hide the qualities nor hide behind them and not fear the reactions of others.

Now you are all constrained enough in your waking state so I expect you to show some freedom in your dream state and to appreciate your freedom. Now there will be, as far as our regular class members are concerned, a particular meeting held that you will attend. Not because I say you will attend it, but because you have already decided to attend it, and I would dearly like to see some memory on the part of the conscious selves involved. There will be some probable selves there, and I would like to introduce you to each other. They will be here at class next week and before then I would like you to have some kind of relationship.

I bid you then a fond good evening, and I wish you this time an active joy.

ESP CLASS SESSION, AUGUST 10, 1971
TUESDAY

(During a class experiment to find the reality of our own probable selves, Seth came through.)

Now I want each of you to examine the feeling, hold the feeling while you listen to me but remember to hold the feeling for they are the connections, these feelings, with parallel selves. Now the feeling should come from the center of the back of your head and extend backward. Do not let my voice take you away from the feeling, but connect you with the feeling.

You can do several things now—walk out of the back of your skull down the path toward the other end. Go out, completely and fully, or if you are pussyfooting, then send your imaginative self out but go.

Now retain the feeling and follow the feeling backward for the feeling itself has smooth sides. Follow it as far as you can and keep your attention clear as to your sensations. Notice particularly whether there is a distant end to this path, and whether there is someone else there, or if it is lighted. If you find others on the path, greet them simply. If you find corridors opening from the path, go down them or not as you feel suited but hold to the feeling that you have.

Now some of you will be able to follow still further, but hold to the feeling. Now I want you to give that feeling freedom to expand, to change into another feeling, for there is for each of you at least one other individual in a parallel existence who is conducting the same experiment that you are conducting now. And the change in that feeling can lead you to the feeling that that other individual is now experiencing.

Now if you are delightfully free, and if you are following, you can follow that path into that other reality and to that other consciousness. Its thoughts and emotions can appear to you. You can, to some extent, or another sense its reality, its subjective vitality.

Now if you are able to go even further imaginatively, you can open those other eyes and look into that other room and that is what I would like you to do. Now for one brief moment I want everyone in this room to open your eyes and then look about the room quickly and close your eyes again. Open your eyes now. Look about. Close your eyes for this other self has also looked out through them.

Now I want you to follow that same path backward entering again through the back of your own skull in which ever way you choose. Use the cricket as a sign, and let it indeed become louder. It belongs to the room in which you will now open your eyes.

Now each of you open your eyes. Now everyone open your eyes.

(When Jane came out of trance she knew some of the students had not returned to the room. Seth returned:)

Examine your own feelings at this time. If you have ever learned the feeling of your own consciousness, learn it now. For to some extent or another, stronger with some of you and weaker in others, you have exchanged with your probable selves, and, in your terms, you are in the wrong room.

Now I want you to follow that channel backward to land in the other room and feel yourselves enter the bodies that sit there. Now the selves that you know are now returning through the channels, and as they do you will experience a relaxation of the neck and shoulder area and as you return into the selves that you know the back of your heads will also feel more rested for the body knew that there was a difference in consciousness for some of you. A touch of an alien nature to which it did not freely respond. Therefore, collect yourselves and now return to this room. And open your eyes.

(Following a discussion of everyone's experience Jane explained a new tenant had moved in and as it was late she would relate what Seth would say.)

What we did tonight is just a starter and *(words missed due to noise)* bugging you to do this, but try and do this in your dreams. Tell yourself before you go to bed that you can do it and then those of you who do stuff during the week, try to do it consciously using the same way we did it tonight. Once you get the feel then you will be able to do it without too much difficulty. And, of course, get all the way back, but I know that's what he was going to say.

I do bid you good evening.

ESP CLASS SESSION, AUGUST 17, 1971 TUESDAY

(Jane said we sounded apprehensive to try any more experiments for awhile. She also gave a few some events that should happen during the week.)

And do not pay any attention to Ruburt when he chews you all out. Simply say that we gave you a rest this week that you sorely needed. My book is finished so I will have plenty of energy left to deal with all of you, and to send you on whatever adventures you are willing to pursue—even our friend, Edgar, over here. Your own fears, however, have a reality and that reality makes itself known.

(To Florence.) Now I want to have a private session with you. Check with Ruburt and I will tell you the time.

Ruburt gave you some idea of some events that in all probability will occur. So I expect you to watch out for them. I will autograph my book for you personally. Now I told you before I began the book that it would be published. I have more confidence than Ruburt has and before I begin my next book, I will let you all know.

Now your probable selves are quite real. They are a part of you. There is no reason to fear them. Does an onion fear its skin or an apple become afraid of its core? Therefore, explore yourself with joy and understanding. There is nothing within you that is so terrible or horrible or sad or misshapen that you dare not face. And this applies to all of you.

(To Maria.) You judged your probable self far too harshly.

(To Ron L.) And our friend, Edgar, judges the self that he knows far too harshly and do not ask me what I mean by the statement.

Now I bid you a fond good evening, and I expect from you all some excellent dream adventures this week into other areas of reality.

(To Derek.) And from you also a more relaxed attitude. Do not worry about physical or nonphysical. Your own being will find its own way within both. You make distinctions that get your back up when there is no reason.

I bid you all, then, a fond good evening. You will read my probable book.

ESP CLASS SESSION, AUGUST 24, 1971
TUESDAY

(Jane asked class to go into Alpha to help a visitor, Juanita, who has ear and eye problems, to help relieve her symptoms. Sue had stated she had an earache.)

Now I want you here where I can see you for a minute *(to Sue)*. And if all of you will listen, in your own way, you can apply what I am about to say to yourselves though for right now I am addressing these two *(Sue and Juanita)*. And I will have something for you all to do later. Now it is a lovely smile. You smile loudly *(to Juanita)*.

Both of you have this thing about noise, and so I will speak to you both at once. And all of you in class did very well. This young man came up with some very good ideas about you as did everyone else in the room. It is only for you now to see and to hear. The world is not as tumultuous as you imagine it to be, and you can hold your own within it. You can, indeed. You can clear your own ears and your own vision. All you have to do is realize that within yourself is the ability to face each life, each day as a life, as you come to it. You are trying too hard now. You must relax and trust the inner self to see and to hear.

The early problems that helped trigger your difficulty you can now, as an adult, overcome these by realizing that the inner self has its own knowledge and its own ways. You can hear me, and I will see to it that you do. Imagine yourself answering questions that have been put to you. You need not imagine that you are hearing clearly. If you imagine that you are answering the questions, then it will be taken for granted that you have heard them correctly. When you try too hard to hear or see, you hear and see less. Relax and let this be taken care of for you. Now you do not trust the inner self to do these things, and you must learn to accept the inner ancient wisdom that is your own.

(To Sue.) And you must learn also that love is noisy

and can be a bother and can get in the way, and you must learn not to deny the validity of your own feelings in those directions where you are now tending to hide them from yourself.

Now each of you, in your own way, hide certain groupings of feelings from yourselves so I am not necessarily directing this specifically at our friend here except that she has the trouble with the ear this evening. The earlier incident, of which you spoke earlier to Ruburt, is connected with this one. And later I will see that Ruburt tells you about it more specifically. For now I will simply tell you that the connection is there. You know that it is, but you must think of what noise represents to you, and what it is that you do not want to hear, and why at this particular time you do not want to hear it.

([Sue:] "Then it's really Sean?")

It is connected with Sean, but it also has deeper roots. I will see that Ruburt tells it to you. This also has to do, however, with the fear of exterior stimuli and the basic fear that it will sweep you away, destroy your person and *(words lost)* of it. You have no security and these thoughts and feelings are highly erroneous. You have physical senses for a reason. They are to help you, not to hinder you. When you refuse to use them for whatever reason, you lessen your own abilities and your own effectiveness as you know, but this is not ever thrust upon you. This is a method of learning, and as you learn you will solve the problem.

I want all of you in this specific case to let out with

the heartiest Mu for our friend here to clear her ears. I will let Ruburt do it, however, because I do not want to huff and puff and blow the roof down. I want that Mu to be as loud and hearty as you can make it, and I want you to take it and joyfully, and let it go through you completely. Not in fear but in joy. Now I want this Mu also to be directed at our friend here *(Sue)* and let them both see that noise can be spiritual and vital and healing and alive and good.

I want you all to Mu for Peter *(Kristof)* who came all across the country.

I will bid you all good evening, but before I do I want you all to know that every teacher, myself included, Edgar, has private projects in which they are very interested and mine happens to be probabilities. Therefore, when you are doing your little experiments in class other teachings are being given to you at the same time that will allow you to more easily contact your probable selves. Now I would like you again to be alert both with the people that you meet during your daily lives and to the people that you meet in the dream state.

(To Sue.) Now you met one particular woman at a supermarket this week, and you do not remember.

([Sue:] "In the dream state?")

In the waking state in a store.

It is within all of your capabilities now to be alert enough in the dream state to recognize these personalities. If you do not recall, upon awakening, them I am now giving you the suggestion that you will recall during the morning as you go about your chores. You have made some excellent advances.

(To Florence.) And you did, dear Lady of Florence, make one this evening.

You are making enough advances so that I expect some more. You are far more lively, even our table moving Edgar over here, in the dream state than you recognize. Now you are having many experiences now that are vital to you in the dream state, and I want you to tell yourself that it is easy to remember them. It is not difficult, it is easy, and you can recall these experiences without effort.

It takes effort to inhibit your memory of your dreams. It is harder to put up that inhibiting factor than it is to simply remember them. So you no longer need to use the effort to inhibit the memory of your dream. You can tell yourselves that you can simply let that effort go. You do not need to use it in that way. Now when you are ready, and it is work in probabilities is a prerequisite, you will be able to meet and remember so that we can carry on class twice a week. And you will only have to pay for once. And you will remember both the location and what you are learning. But it is not handed out to you on a silver platter. Your own abilities operate here, but this is within your reach now.

(To Ron) It is not within your reach now, but they will carry you along. Until you learn to laugh inside. I will give you laughing sessions. The gods all laugh, they have no time for seriousness.

Then those of you who are adventurous can begin to embark on some night time experiences such as you have never remembered before. This can start now, and for some of you it will. Now I want each of you to put your notebook, each of you, to put your notebook by your bedside. And tell Ruburt he is no exception. Now explorers must keep records, and you are all explorers, and we draw our black sheep of the universe from all directions.

(To Sue.) What Ruburt told you was correct as far as it went.

Now I want to see each of you follow those directions as well, of course, as those directions given earlier by Ruburt for our beanstalk here. We want him healthy, strong, glowing and laughing. I expect your adventures to begin this evening.

(To Juanita.) And I hope I scared you enough so that you will hear and see. Nothing can be louder than I am so if you are not afraid of this sound, there is no need for you to be afraid of the sound of your fellows.

(Very softly) You know what I am about to do because I know what Ruburt knows, that our friend upstairs is not upstairs. Now then I want you to do something else.

(Very loudly) As you sense the energy within this voice grab a hold of it, use it for your own purposes. Realize that as it flows through this figure so indeed can it flow through your own. And it does. You do not need to translate it into sound. Translate it into health and

vitality and laughter. Use it as you will but realize it is your own, and that within you there is a source of such vitality and strength. Realize also that physical existence is good. It is blessed. It is in your terms real, and it is meant for you. It is your medium of expression. Feel free in it. Enjoy it.

I bid you all a fond good evening, and I expect to see you floating like little ghosties out of your bodies this evening. I will be like a pied piper leading all of you in a toottoottoot and no one will shoot us down. They are trying.

My heartiest good wishes to you all and a fond good evening.

ESP CLASS SESSION, AUGUST 31, 1971
TUESDAY

(During a discussion of students experiences for the week.)

You mean when we were Muing. Muing is good for the constitution and even better for the soul. Now I am not going to interrupt until you are all finished but I could not keep out of that one. You are all doing very well. You are supporting yourselves in the dream state. You are relating in new ways and you are relating in different ways in class. I simply wanted you to know that I was here and that I am listening. And I am glad to see that everyone remembered to bless our friend, Edgar.

(Jane told about seeing the cloudlike formation.)

Now you form the physical image that you know unconsciously. Because you see it in a mirror and experience its reality you take it for granted that it is real. Even our friend, Edgar, believes that he has a physical body. As I told you I have some difficulty at times explaining to my own friends that you so believe such a hallucination is real. There are other portions of your reality also formed by your thoughts and emotions however, that are not so obvious to you. You are not aware of them and so you do not accept them as a portion of your own experience and yet they do exist. I am not referring now simply to probable selves. I am referring to what you may call freewheeling energy that you release filled with your own intent and emotional coloration which has a reality in other spheres beside your own. This reality acts within the physical fear though its main existence is not within it. It has therefore an electromagnetic effect within your system although you cannot perceive it physically. It is a psychological reality or a psychic one if you prefer. Now each of you, to some extent or another, build up such forms as you may refer to them. They are conscious. All form has consciousness. You give birth to them automatically. They are a product of your own psychic and mental and psychological activity and so they exist whether or not you perceive them. They are extensions of you from your point of view. They can almost be considered as extra perceptive mechanisms that

SESSION 8/31/1971

exist apart from the physical one. They formed through concentrations of energy. Now when you use all of your energy to manipulate in the physical reality there is little left to form such images. When you learn through relaxation to accept life spontaneously and to trust to your own inner being then this energy is released. You become, therefore, more effective.

Our regular students have been experiencing an extra bonus. You are beginning your own dream classes as you know. Some of you already know the evenings in which you will work and the area in which you will be involved. As you learn to live spontaneously on a physical level, so automatically you will be able to build up such forms and when you do you must learn to train them. You have hands and you have to learn how to use them when you are a child. And so when you grow these forms you must learn how to use them with respect and love. Those of you who have already experienced their first extracurricular class should have the second installment this week and those of you who lag behind should begin your first installment. Ruburt has an experiment in mind however and so I will wait and see how you do. My heartiest welcome to visitors for the evening.

(Sue used the term thought forms in explaining to Jane what Seth had said.)

They are energy forms rather than thought forms. There is a difference.

([Wally:] "Thoughts have energy, Seth.")

But energy forms depend upon strong, very powerful

concentrations of energy whether thought or emotion is involved. These are in your terms, excesses of energy that shoot out from you like stars but coalesce into a shape and a form. They are usually the result of, in your terms, a long term build up of energy although the same effect can be reached by one extremely powerful image or thought. There is however a difference. Now I have always referred to myself as a personality energy essence because it was true and also because it sounded very safe to Ruburt. You could not argue against it. He did not have to say that I said I was a spirit or I was some sort of a White God or that I was an illuminati. The term was simple and he could accept it. It is a lovely term if I do say so myself. I will stick with it always. I will see that Ruburt puts it in his introduction.

(Following an experiment to find other probable selves.)

You are all multidimensional realities. You are learning to use your consciousness to become conscious cocreators of your own reality. Some of you this evening, after class, will be involved in some adventures that I hope you will remember.

Now I am going to ask you once again to close your eyes to follow me to the best of your ability. You do not have to follow me to the best of your ability. You do not have to follow me and visitors here this evening do not have to feel as if they must follow me. Allow yourselves the freedom not to follow me if you do not feel like it. Others of you allow yourself the freedom to follow me. Now regular class members are aware of the way in which I use this voice. I want you then to realize that the energy within it also is the energy within you. That is, you have the same energy within you, if you decide to use it you can do so. I use it only to show you that it is also available to you. I want you then to translate the sound of the voice into intensities of different kinds of perception. I want you to use the energy behind the voice to remind yourself of your own energy. I want you to open yourselves to the realization that you are multidimensional and to experience this multidimensionality in personal terms, not theoretically. I want you then to have an emotional experience in which if even only for a moment, you experience the fullness and vitality of your own nature and of your own identity. I want you to feel within yourself your own abilities and energy and power. I want you to feel it so strongly that the realization and the intimate knowledge will remain within you. Now even as this voice grows stronger let the feelings within yourselves grow stronger and let you feel your own energy from the inner self fill your consciousness and your physical being with vitality and knowledge and the joy of existence. Let the sound of the voice, therefore, bring out in yourselves the power of your own identity and independence, the integrity of your own being. Let it bring within you the memory of all yourselves. Let you then awaken to the selves that you are now. Let you become aware of your own parts, let the separated areas within your personalities awaken to themselves and join forces. Let the power and vitality and creativity of the inner self within you fill you now with knowledge and creativity and the joy and essence of vitality. Let it ring throughout the cells of your body and dance within the cells of your brain. Let it uplift your spirit. Let it give you, indeed, a vitality and strength that will remain within you personally with which you can identify and let it lead you directly to the inner selves that are your own. And now with a whisper I leave you to yourselves. Open your eyes to the room and to the time that you know but feel that vitality and know it is your own. And when you are dead as I have been, in your terms, for all this time I hope you can yell as lustily as I can.

([Jane:] "I know that he did something, Mary.

(To Mary Ellen.) Explain what I did.

(Mary Ellen recapped Seth's previous comments for Jane.)

JANE'S EXERCISE IN CLASS AUGUST 31, 1971

Seth has gone into these coordination points, and told... well, you don't know what they are, do you? No. Never mind. Okay. The experiment that I've got in mind is some more of this stuff going out the back, because I think we've done a great job of that, and I feel it's quite significant. Because we did it in a Creative Writing class without making any suggestions as to what we would meet, or rather than probable selves or anything, I'm going to suggest tonight that we do it with that in mind.

Already I have the feeling... yeah, okay, so I ask everybody that wants to, close your eyes, since that seems to be easiest. Hopefully, get comfortable.

SESSION 8/31/1971

Those of you who are new, just consider it as an adventure in consciousness and see what you can do with it. We close our eyes simply because it's easier. I suggest that you close your eyes then. Those of you who are regular members of the class should have no difficulty in feeling that sensation that we get out of the back of our heads as if a pyramid were opening up.

I would like all of you to give yourself full freedom as far as perception is concerned. If you feel this particular sensation in the back of your head, you can just follow it. If you don't, imagine the pyramid, the angle going out into a path that extends behind you. Those of you that have been involved in this before have simply to send your consciousness out through that pyramid so that it finds its own adventures. The others do this imaginatively.

Imagine yourself walking out, perhaps as a miniature person, out of this pyramid. If you want you can stop and look back even, at the back of your head. I really believe, and most of the people in the class do, that there are dimensions of consciousness that are open to us if we only try. And that this is one. And that this particular journey of consciousness, we are leaving ourselves completely open to experience to whatever happens without making any demands or suggestions.

Follow down the path then. If for you the image becomes different or if you're doing your own thing, that's great, then follow it, and simply use my voice as a yardstick, as something to connect you to the room. Those who are following the pyramid will find hopefully, that they can travel down it easily; that it extends adjacently to our usual level of experience.

There's a door at the other end and that it can be easily

opened. If you find your consciousness aware of other things, then follow those things but allow it its natural freedom and use it. Unfocus your attention in the usual physical environment in which you're involved. Your consciousness is like a light for you to use. Then use it freely. Look in other areas of perception than those you usually pursue. You may perceive colors. You may see people. You may see a scene. You may simply be involved in kinetic sensation. But whatever it is follow it and allow yourself the freedom to do so.

You may find that the pyramid itself changes its dimensions. There's a top that opens or a bottom that opens, or a room that opens from either side. Feel free to explore whatever you find. And by all means enjoy the feeling of your own consciousness as it does these things.

Consciousness has a feel the same way that a body does. When you do different things with it, it feels differently. The feelings themselves can be clues, so that when you feel them again they're familiar. Consciousness isn't solid, airy, distant thing that you just see through. It's an alive, vital part of us. It provides various kinds of sensation. It's free outside of the body, sometimes freer than it is inside the body. Therefore let it find its own way in this experiment. Let it go wherever it wants. Give it the same kind of a freedom that you would if you were holding a flashlight and flashing it through a forest. You wouldn't say I'll only flash the light in this direction because it's a safe direction. You'd flash it all over so that you could see what was before you. Usually we just flash our consciousness in one direction and say this is real, but in this experiment at least, let us flash that light down that pyramid in whatever direction we choose.

Open thresholds that we'll remember. If we feel new sensations or perceptions all the better. Realize, as best as you can individually, that you are not your consciousness. Your consciousness is yours for you to use. And use it gladly. Your consciousness is merely one more of your abilities. Give it freedom. Let it bring you clues as to the nature of reality. You don't have to make any judgments. This is like taking snapshots of a strange land.

So don't make judgments from what you see. Or what you hear, or what you feel. All I know, that within and beyond and through the world that we know, there are other levels of reality, other dimensions of activity, other psychological gestalts that we can explore. Allow yourself the full freedom to do this. I'm going to be quiet for a moment in which time you can explore what you are experiencing. And then use my voice as a cord to bring you back to your normal perception. But in the meantime take advantage of the opportunikty to allow your consciousness its freedom.

Now begin to return. Begin to return your consciousness back down the pyramid to the room. The feeling connected with the back of your head should become stronger as you come back toward the self that you know, and the perceptions that are so familiar. Return gladly to the kind of perception that you always knew. Return to the body that is so secure and willing. Return gladly to the physical form that is a vehicle for your expression in this time and this place. Return to the time and the place gladly, the way someone returns to home, but knowing in the back of your mind that there are many homes and many places and many times, but for now return your focuses, settling back gladly into the body. The consciousness returning once again to the beautiful ivory bone skull, the eyes opening into the ordinary room.

JANE ROBERTS' ESP CLASS, AUGUST 31, 1971 TUESDAY

Jane: What I imagine is that in Creative Writing class which consists here today of two people, Charlie's mother, and Hope W., who is a young gal or a gal in, I don't know how old, 30 maybe, no, 28. I don't know.

Anyway, we do different things in that class and one of the things that we did, you know how we in this class use the pyramid at the top of the head to contact other probable selves? Well, in that class I suggested that we use the pyramid and I didn't give them any suggestions as to what they might come up with, but just that they send their consciousness out. And they did get the feeling that we do get when we're doing it here. And it only took maybe 3,4 minutes. That they send their consciousness out and just accept whatever they got. They got the pyramid effect, the path, the whole bit that we get.

Frances got something I thought was quite nice. She found a woman talking to her and giving her information and knew that she could get this at just about anytime. Hope found herself in a fantastic meadow, you know, serene, everything was just great. A place of great peace, and knew that she could go there anytime she wanted. That week for me had been hectic in that more than usual I was getting telephone calls....

.... With the Black Thing, those of you who remember the Seth Material *and the Black Thing, which was representative of my fears at that time and that I had created them and reacted to them. Well, helper is the opposite, sort of. According to what we got last night and this is just a preliminary, the helper is sort of made up of a surplus of positive energy, the desire to help people and so forth; but the best, plus, parts of your personality.*

According to what we got, both the Black Thing and the helper only exist when you have the kind of personality or the kind of abilities or something that draw a lot of energy where you got it to use. Otherwise the effects just aren't that obvious, though they are there. That the helper is consciousness, that is it does have a consciousness that I have released. That it represent the best things I hope to do. That it is learning and that I have to train it. Okay about sending it out to Sue and showing it how to do things or telling it how to do things and it learns as it goes along. That it's like an appendage, a psychic appendage that is highly beneficial that you build up and can use and so I've been trying to do this.

The effect leads to all kinds of things. You can look at this, the whole phenomena, anyway you want. You can call it the Black Thing. I don't know if you got that far in the book yet?

(Student:) No, I didn't.

Jane: Okay, you can call it the dark side of the personality and you can compare, if you just look at it that way, the helper with the bright side of the personality if you want. You can experiment. With others you can get an idea for things in class that you can do on your own. But if you don't spend the time to do it on your own, you won't get results. So it's up to you as to how much time you want to spend. And how curious you are to use your abilities to find out what you can do with your own consciousness. 'Cause each of you can do different things with your consciousness than I can do with mine, because your consciousness is your own. Your experiences are going to be your own. You'll be as free with them as you allow yourselves to be. I think that what you're doing in the dream state, with what some of us are doing, is really great. I think it's a breakthrough. And I think that if we continue that we'll really have some fantastic things going for us. And when I talk now I'm (words lost)... is that I'm also sending stuff out to some of the regular members in class who are working hard and to whom I dont have time to speak in class. And I found out on building up this helper, you're all building up also your own helpers in those terms, that you can use. I think that before we finish all the regular class members will be having dream experiences that are as vivid as what goes on in regular class. And that your daily lives will be immeasurably enriched. I think, see, personally because of the way I work in conscious writing, that your own consciousness is such a fantastic, precious thing; and to close it in is... I just can't understand it. That you should allow yourself every ability you can to see what you can do with it.

And if you get various kinds of hangups then you'll get over them. I think that Ron has got some, Florence has got some. We all have some to various degrees. But you can work through them, and I'd really like all of you to do this. I'm sorry to say that Florence will not be able to come to class next week, so I suggest that we take Sue, instead of Ron or Florence, and all work on Sue this week. So that we can work on Florence in the time when she'll be here the next week to report and know what's going on. and I want you to take particular note with your dreams. And try, 'cause I know you can all do it, to take your conscious awareness into the dream state. It's not that difficult. It's just difficult because you think it is. And really see what you can do, 'cause you can do stuff in the dream state with your consciousness just like you can here. You just have to realize you can do it. And I'm saying good night for Seth and that means class is over.

(Student:) *"This going to be my last class."*

Jane: Alright.

(Student:) *"I'm making plans to move."*

Jane: Where are you moving?

(Student:) *"I've got a couple of jobs lined up. Possibly in the Syracuse area. I haven't made a final decision yet."*

Jane: We want a good Mu for those people that are leaving. Alright. You're sure of that, right?

(Class:) Mu!

ESP CLASS SESSION, SEPTEMBER 7, 1971
TUESDAY

Now I wanted to say a few words and he is worried about the gentleman upstairs and wants me to keep my voice down. It is difficult for me to keep my voice down when my old friend is over there *(Rachel Clayton)*, and if it were not too late I would have you all Mu a good loud and cheery Mu. Sometime I will show you how to do a whispered Mu. Believe it or not, it is more difficult.

Now, good evening to you *(Brad Lanton)* and welcome, and welcome to our guests here. Now what I want you to do is this. It is late, so we will only have a trial run. This will be in Alpha state, so close your eyes and I will give you a lullaby.

Now imagine anything that you choose but have a line or a platform that represents Alpha I. Have it in your mind as a symbol of adjacent consciousness at the same level, perhaps, as your eyes. Do whatever you choose. Imagine yourself as a small figure on the line, for example. Imagine a road and yourself upon it. Now I will want you shortly to imagine other such lines or roads, so pick an image for yourself, that you can use. See yourself clearly on this line or road or path. You may use a floor if you prefer, but see yourself upon it, for this will represent A-I.

Now imagine another adjacent road or line parallel and still further away from your normal consciousness. Now pause to feel the difference in your consciousness as you move from one line or road to another. And this one represents A-II.

Now imagine again a third line or path, still parallel and adjacent. Examine the feel of your consciousness as you do so. Move now, further on this time, to another path or road that you will call A-IV, and that is still further in distance from your normal consciousness. Now imagine still another line which we will call A-V.

Now here, pause for a moment. If you can, imaginatively look behind you to see these other four roads or paths that run adjacently and parallel. Now turn, step back to the previous road or path to A-IV. Step again back to A-III. Step again back to A-II. Now carefully step back to A-I and pause. Feel your own consciousness at this point.

And now imagine a step <u>above</u> A-I. Not adjacent or parallel, but above, and feel yourself step up upon it. And we will call it A-I-a, though the names make little difference. Pause there and imaginatively look down to A-I, but hold your position.

Now above you, you will see another step. Go up this step again and notice the changes in the feel of yourself and of your consciousness. You will find another step. Step up this one, noticing again any change in the feel of yourself or in your consciousness. Above this is still another. Now step up here and pause.

Imaginatively look down. Look at the other levels of consciousness from which you have come. Now very slowly, come back to the previous level, and keep coming down each step slowly until you reach again the original A-I from which you began.

Now, at A-I, realize that all these other levels of consciousness are also available from that threshold, and later you will be instructed more clearly as to their use. For now, however, simply acquaint yourself with the feeling of A-I as a threshold of activity, as a doorway into other kinds of perception and consciousness.

Now, very gently step from A-I back to your normal state of consciousness and open your eyes.

(To Bette.) The love was too much, you see.

Now I will let Ruburt return.

(Peter K. explained the above to Jane.)

Now this is the equivalent of scales. So I want you all to practice on your own. I will not say that practice makes perfect, but at least it gives you a chance.

(Class discussed the exercise and how our consciousness changed.)

Now, I bid you all a fond good evening. But I want you to try these exercises as you fall to sleep at night, and you will have some excellent projections. You will also have some other experiences, so I suggest that you try these at that time. You may prolong the time, you see. We did this quickly this evening.

(To Rachel C.) And I have been over to see you if you have not been over to see me.

([Rachel:] "I knew you were over, Seth. Thank you.")

If I had not said so, she would not have mentioned it.

SESSION 9/14/71

There are some <u>people</u> looking about for some other people to guide in the dream state. And I would like to see you all get together. Regular class members know what I am speaking of. You can all have your helpers. You do not have to find them, but let them find you.

Now I suggest that you end class, if you can do it, with a whispered Mu for the much-loved one over in the corner *(Bette)*.

ESP CLASS SESSION, SEPTEMBER 14, 1971 TUESDAY

I will shortly let you take your class break. I have a few remarks, however. I would like to compliment your fantastic memories. On that particular Saturday evening you were all involved in the same dream experience, but each of you received your own messages. Some of you did not even remember that the messages had been given. Our cousin of Richelieu over here, however, did, and the message was repeated the following evening with a noted lack of success as far as memory was concerned. Each of you, however, received information, and some of you are acquainted with some of your probable selves.

Now before we go into the messages that you were given, I give my warmest welcome over here to our renegade from New York and this jailbird over here in the corner.

(To Arnold.) And my congratulations here to our

African God for the dream which was indeed quite significant.

(To Joel.) You know I am going to say this to our friend of the idiot flowers over there. You are progressing well on your own, and the information that you are receiving is basically correct.

Now the dream state does indeed involve an acceleration. And according to the experiences that you have various rates are involved.

I do not want these two newcomers over here to feel left out, so I will say welcome to both of you.

(To Dee G.) And it is far better to look within yourself for answers than to receive them from the outside.

(To Hope W.) I like someone in the class named Hope. We must get a Faith and a Charity.

([Joel:] "I was thinking about this acceleration. Today I went out in the back where we have the tent for Peter, and I was lying down and thinking and I started to hear this beep-beep-beep kind of sound and looked, and it wasn't coming from anything around. Then I remembered having heard this in that same place in the yard a couple of times before while also lying down and being in sort of a psy-time state, and I just began to get some ideas now that this might in some way be related to the discussion.")

It is not related specifically to the discussion of acceleration. It is indeed related, however, to your own experience. This is merely a clue to you, and you should receive it in other locations also. And it is a signal to you that other information is coming through and can be perceived. Now in your particular case the information can be perceived at such instances through focusing upon the physical object closest to you and then nonfocusing. Do you follow me? I will not tell you ahead of time what experience you can expect but follow through upon the next instance as I suggest.

([Gert:] "On this crocodile business, was this reincarnational material?")

This was reincarnational material.

([Gert:] "Did I follow it through?")

You did indeed, but do not be so intent upon putting a symbolic meaning upon the crocodile for it was quite real.

([Gert:] "I felt that very much. I did not make it the first time?")

You did not.

([Gert:] "But when I went through, in other words what I was doing …. ")

What you were doing was making the previous personality very happy. Your daydream was not only your daydream but his.

Now if you have not already discovered it for yourselves, and some of you have, you have visitors here this evening. And see that you treat them well. You have also had visitors in one of your class dreams.

Now see what you can do with the acceleration now and how far you can follow it. And each of you in your own way see how you can sense the acceleration and if you can fly along on Ruburt's coattails. He will indeed, as he mentioned last night, take you on a piggyback ride. In your own way then translate the acceleration and see where it brings you and how far your consciousness can go with it before you become dizzy and how far back you can look and how far forward and how far and how deeply into yourself you can look. And when you look deeply into yourself where does this lead you? And what other paths lead you forever outward and outward into what realities that bring you once again inward? Then sense the acceleration, and see what you can do with it and use it in your own way for the voice is also a symbol of that acceleration as well as the energy. Shortly Ruburt will be able to use the volume also in other ways, but now you can use it and piggyback ride upon it and see where it will take you. You must not, however, feel insecure but safe and you must also feel adventurous.

Our friend here of the idiot flower, then look through and beyond Ruburt's head and wherever that leads you then follow and follow in your own way.

And feel your own energy now rise and accelerate. We will give you a quick lesson. Feel it rise up ever quicker and faster. Let the experience be your own and let it bring you in whatever direction that it can. Do not stop yourself or question or wonder. Simply follow it as you would a wind, let it carry you wherever it will. Simply to get used to the feeling and sensation. And now ever so gently let it bring you back down. You must fall down with it for you cannot descend slowly.

Now take your break.

(Jane said goodnight for Seth.)

ESP CLASS SESSION, SEPTEMBER 21, 1971
TUESDAY

Now I call an end to break. I do not want our friend here *(Martin Crocker)* to feel as he feels that he is cramping your style. Now I have one remark. There is an incident in your life, and it did indeed have to do with the use of inner perception. It was not therefore an ordinary event in usual terms. There was also another person connected with the affair who telepathically knew what was going on, and in his own way helped bring about the events and communicated them to you.

Now as Ruburt said earlier, he *(Martin)* is a good man and besides that I like him. Now he may not approve of Ruburt's habits, but then Ruburt does not approve of his, and that is between he and Ruburt. As you are all used to saying, you must do your own thing in your own way. There are distortions in his thought as there are distortions in all of your thoughts. He thinks of vitality in different ways than you do, but he uses it very well. Now when the myths speak, they speak with many voices. You must indeed look beneath them, and you must learn to listen to the inner voice within that is not fooled by any myths. Now the vitality that is within him is expressed in a different way than you express your own and the terms attached to it. And the tales that go along with it are different than your own. But the true reality cannot be put into words. Neither words within your brain, within your mind; for the voice itself and language itself is bound to be distorted. The words are merely symbols for the reality. You need the words in your state of being but only each of you in your own way can search for the reality that has no need of words. The reality that needs no sound. And when the speakers speak to each of you in the dream state and in your private hours then they do not need words. You translate what they say into words, but the inner knowledge within you exists long before any alphabet was ever known. The inner knowledge within you existed before the nervous system existed, before there was a brain capable of learning language. And so let the inner energy and vitality then rise up and express itself. And open up those doors of energy. Do not close them down. All of the myths should float away, and all the debris. A man's myths are like his clothing they are his own affair. Beneath the clothing is the person and the reality. And now I will let you take your break. A Seth break and a class break.

(After break.) All right now, the experiment that began some time ago is still in operation and the visitors that come here do not come here by chance alone.

(To Martin) Now what I said to you earlier did not refer to the meeting. It referred to another situation privately in your own life. There was however some recognition in that you were a woman back in the 16th century in Spain and someone I knew, knew you then and so

there is some point of contact.

Now the channels this evening to probable selves are open rather clearly. I would like you to follow then, to close your eyes. Now concentrate on the feeling in the back of your skull. The feeling is the important thing for from it the pyramid shape will of itself form. Now feel the pyramid and be aware of it. It will be different to each of you, for it is your own personal path into probable realities. I want you then, freely, to follow through it. Use my voice simply as a thread so that you can follow it, and it can bring you back safely but concentrate upon your own feelings and sensations. You should find the pyramid forming easily. It may seem as a path or a ray of light but follow it with full freedom and confidence.

Now to our Lady of Florence in particular, let me add feelings of strength and freedom to you so that you feel free to pursue this particular path.

Outward from your skulls, therefore, into a dimension that has no space or time, in your terms. See this pyramid extending, and whatever you find within it meet freely and with confidence. If there are rooms, then pursue them. If you see a particular person then speak or make yourself known. If you find another group of people, then relate to them in whatever way seems natural. If instead the distance seems immeasurable and the way long, then follow it. Now you are seated physically in a particular room upon an autumn night and yet these pyramids extend where seasons are not known and where autumn nights are not known and you are traveling on paths between dimensions. Therefore free your perceptions while you have the opportunity and use your consciousness naturally in the way that it is meant for you to use it, freely and with confidence and joy. Be assured of your own vitality and your own confidence to deal with all situations. Let my voice then serve even to form a portion of the pyramid so that you have even greater feelings of support. Whatever scenes come, follow them. Whatever thoughts come, follow them. Whatever rooms open, explore them. Whatever sensations you have, accept them joyfully and with confidence. Learn to use the mobility of your own consciousness joyfully and follow even further into the pyramid and into, indeed, the light of consciousness and understanding, for it reaches as a pathway between those dimensions, and it is indeed a channel between those dimensions, and it is indeed a channel between your world and other worlds that also exist. I want you then to draw energy and power from the voice and use it in your own way. Let it become whatever you want it to become and whatever you need it to become in this particular time, in this particular place in this particular probability system in which you find yourself. And if you find another self, then greet it. And if you see another face, then give a look of recognition. And if you find another brush past you then wish it well. And if you find worlds that you do not understand, then look upon them with wonder, but send your consciousness as far as it can go with great vigor, with freedom and joy. Let it go where it wants to go and travel those pathways that are native to it, that are as native to it as breath is to your physical body. Let yourself then be flooded with comprehension and with knowledge and let all those intuitive connections be made that need to be made. Let other probable selves help you as indeed you aid them. And let the self that you know realize its potential and part of All That Is. And now for the last spurt let your consciousness go still further so that you know you are sending it as far as you can, that you are using it clearly and with vigor.

And stop where you are and look and feel and listen. Let whatever truths come to you be comprehended. Whatever scene you see, remember it. Whatever words you hear, remember those. Send your consciousness then into those dimensions that are yours by right. Let your consciousness indeed take wing. Use its abilities. *(Long pause.)*

(Very softly.) And now quietly return away from where you have been. Turn and return again through to the pyramid and the channel, back through to the rooms and the scenes and past people. Return again to the seasons, to the autumn, to the earth and the physical universe that you know. Return again thankfully and with joy to the self that you know, to the body that you know, and feel the energy flood through your physical being and open your eyes to the room and to the people that you know.

(Discussion of everyone's personal experiences.)

Our cousin of Richelieu *(Bette)* over here should have a meeting with an old friend in the dream state this evening, so remember. And your other friend is due back for some more projection work this week.

And the others of you will find your dream nights stabilizing. Your dream classes, therefore, will become more clear. The experiment that began as I said is still continuing and some of this will also appear in your dream state. Some other clues, however, will appear when you are wide awake and going about your daily ways so keep good notes this week and you also. Some other events that we have been working toward are close to fruition and next week you may find yourselves realizing what these are. Also be on the lookout for strangers that specifically approach you. Not strangers that you meet, but strangers that approach you where no effort is required on your part. This in connection with other people that you have known. So I expect you will have a busy week and I also expect that we will have a busy class next week. If certain watchers are watching you, as I have said before, there is no reason why you cannot watch them also. So keep your eyes open.

I bid you all a fond good evening and prepare to be adventurous this week. You have the tendency to rest after you have been doing well for a time, but the period of rest is over. Now your periods do not always match. Our Cousin over here, for example, has had a rather active week.

(To Arnold.) I would like you to do some more writing, for you will have results from that if you continue with it faithfully.

Now I bid you all a fond good evening, and those blessings that I have to give I give you, and those blessings that I do not have to give you you know where you will have to ask for them. And if you are looking for vitality, look to the inner self and you will find it. And learn to accelerate your own thoughts.

ESP CLASS SESSION, OCTOBER 5, 1971
TUESDAY

(Seth had given instructions on relating to our past and present selves. After a pause, Janice Simmonds said, in a tiny choked voice, "I don't belong here. I want to go home." She looked over at Phil Levine and said, "What did you do to me?" and she started to cry.

(Jane told Phil that Janice had been his wife in Persia about ten centuries ago. Janice cried again, "Why did you do it? Why did you leave me?"

(Jane said, "It's all right, Janice," and then said to Phil, "There was a baby. I don't want to do this for you, see. I want you to do it, just comfort her and don't worry about it."

(Phil went over to Janice and they embraced, "I won't leave you again; I want to stay this time," Phil said. Finally, Phil sat down. Someone remarked that he was getting it with both barrels tonight. He and Janice talked about how they had each felt something in common with the other when Phil first came to class. Janice said she had distrusted Phil at first but felt better about it now.

(Suddenly, Jane said to Phil, "Tell her about the journey you took, Phil, the journey!" Phil looked confused.

("You took a journey by boat," Jane said. "By boat, that's what it was and you left her, and she wants to understand why you left and you know why."

(Phil said, "I don't think I can tell her."

("You mean after ten centuries you can't tell your own wife?" Jane said, "now isn't that carrying things a bit too far? Of all people, why couldn't you tell her after all this time?"

(Phil hesitated and said, "I think I wanted to go off with someone else, but I didn't want to leave you and I couldn't tell you," and stopped awkwardly. Janice started to cry again.

("I want to come back to you now," Phil said to Janice.

("But you can't. It's too late," Janice said. "It must stay in the past."

(Garbled conversation here. Phil and Janice say something about accepting each other as they are now.

(Suddenly Jane leaned forward and said, "I got the idea—I was getting this the name Bando Bah Zahyar Dhar... sacrificed the baby to a goddess in Persia. A goddess that you followed...She [Janice] was left screaming. The goddess' name, I think; I never heard of anything like this, was something like Von Bazelraeha.. and they killed the children ...400 children one afternoon ...400 children in one day, and that baby was one of them. Sethpherverando was the name for the baby ...I'm getting the scene and I don't want to get into the emotional end, so I keep cutting that off to just give you the information.

("This goddess was the goddess of fertility...and you were

from a province in Persia ...You were both poor ...Province was called Sepharthein in the southwest portion of Persia... It was a national holiday, sacrificial day ...something that we would translate into atonement but that wasn't the word at all ...where children were sacrificed, so that the earth would grow ... You [Phil], that's why you hit her [Janice] so strongly. You looked something like you do now, only your build was scrawnier. You lived in a mud-type hut ... You had other wives afterwards ...I'm trying to get something you can check, but it's so long ago you can't ...but the emotion is fantastic. She didn't want you to take the baby, and you just took it. And this was supposed to make you wealthy. If you gave the baby it was supposed to make you really wealthy. It was supposed to do all kinds of fantastic things; and it <u>didn't, it didn't, it didn't!</u> ...And you didn't have the guts to go back ...and you wandered, and you wandered alone, because you didn't have the guts to go back. And all you had was a cut—a wound in your left thigh. You were kicked by the mob, because after you threw in your baby boy, nobody gave a damn. It was just this fantastic mob ...and those kids were cooked...and it was all in the name of religion and in the name of all this stuff except that out of it you hoped to get wealth ...and all she [Janice] had was a woman's common love for the child. She tried to hold it, and it meant nothing. Shortly after, an army came down, of stragglers, in that area; and they were hungry ... They were stragglers from another country and they didn't have any food and they were disbanded.. And they burned everything they saw and took what they could take and that's what they did... and you

[Phil] never knew, never went back, and you're meeting Pete K. now ...and I'm trying like hell to cut the emotion part out 'cause I don't want to get into..." [Jane stops here.]

(Janice said she felt Pete was that baby, and all three agree he was.

(We had been discussing Gert and Phil's recollections.)

Now for a few words from me. And first of all, to show you what a polite host I am, I bid our evening guests welcome, and I do not mean to exclude you. My first words, however, are for a few of these people over here.

As I told you often, no matter where you come from, and no matter what years you think you inhabit, it is no coincidence that you have gathered here. And as many of you come and go, so have you come and gone in other times and places. And you will indeed work out dramas in what you think of as this room, and by working out these dramas, you change events both in your past and in your future, for time is open-ended.

Now I am going to do something here if you want to do it, and you must be brave and adventurous, and I am sure that you all are *(much laughter)*. As I speak, I want you to allow and encourage—actively encourage—other selves that you have known. Let them come to the surface. Be aware within yourself of subjective feelings, emotions, or thoughts that may not be those that you identify with yourself in this time. They may be directed to others in the room. They may have no connection to others in the room; but I want *(shouts)* you to use the energy behind this voice for your own purposes. Let it call up from your own bank of personalities both those people that you may have been in those terms; those people that you are; those strangers that you are and do not recognize; or those selves that you may be in years to come. And let them, then, mingle in your own consciousness and become a part of what you are. Let your consciousness expand and say, "here, counterparts, I accept you—in love, in knowledge, and in understanding. Therefore, let me know what you are, and let me become a part of all that I am. Let this knowledge come, then, into my consciousness, let me be no longer divided."

(Still shouting) I want you to feel the energy that is yourself rise up from the depths of your being and merge with the consciousness that you know; *(quietly)* and when my voice ceases its words, then I expect a spontaneous encounter with yourself and those portions of yourself that you do not recognize, and with others in the room. Say what comes into your minds; what impressions come, accept them. Let the room, therefore, be a meeting place of selves, a gathering together of selves from many times and places. Let the secrets of your selves come into your knowledge and into what you think of as this time and place, and let all portions of your personality therefore unite and meet here. Let there be a convention of selves from all places and times. Let this moment, then, be a center to which other portions of the self come and greet each other and say, "Hello, brothers, you are

myself."

Now I want you to open your eyes and look about, to say those words that are on your lips, to unite with strong emotion and in most real and valid terms, in tears or in laughter, even in anger, in all those fresh, lively emotions that have their counterparts in many worlds.

ESP CLASS SESSION, OCTOBER 19, 1971 TUESDAY

(Dee G. asked how one looks for reality inside oneself.)
If you look outward, then you see what you have created, all of you.

Now, my welcome to those who came for the evening, and I have a few remarks to make to our regular class members. You have met many strangers lately, both in the dream state and in regular waking reality. And you met some strangers here last week. See that you learn who they were.

Some of you were quite surprised by the strangers that you met. None of you have made the connections as yet between the strangers you have met in your dreams, the strangers that have come to class, and your own experiences.

(To Bette.) There is also someone, my dear cousin of Richelieu, you forgot in your out-of-body state. Ask your friend who you met that you have forgotten.

Now all of this correlates ever since we began the

experiment, and you do indeed have a purpose this evening.

Now, I would like all of you to try this with me. Imagine *(to Kris)* and even you imagine your own consciousness accelerated, faster and faster and faster. Now, close your eyes if it suits you. And if it does not suit you, leave them open. Use my voice again, simply to give you something to hang on to, and translate the tones into the acceleration of your own consciousness, and translate the energy so you can use it to form your own path. And follow the acceleration of your own consciousness gladly and joyfully and openly and follow it wherever it wants to go, freely, in gratitude. Let the energy, therefore, of my voice serve as steps or pathways, whatever you desire, to lead you wherever your inner self desires to go. And know that you will return to the room, that the physical image is still within it, but allow yourself the freedom to travel between dimensions, to accept what comes to you gladly, even our Lady of Florence over there in the corner; to open up joyfully and follow, *(to Florence)* and you close your eyes.

I want you to travel as far inward as you have ever traveled outward. I want you to travel further than you have gone before, to open up yourself with greater freedom and joy to other forms of consciousness that are your own; to other roads that exist for you, to other kinds of knowledge that you either may or may not be able to verbalize.

(Very loud.) I want you to climb the vowels and syl-

lables of this voice as if they were indeed a ladder, and let them carry you into dimensions that are native to you, dimensions that are yours by right, that are your heritage; *(really booming)* dimensions of awareness that you carry within you both day and night, beneath the level of your ordinary days. I want you to feel that energy that belongs to you, that knowledge that is a part of your genes, that fills yourselves with acceleration and joy and exaltation. *(Emphasizes every word.)* And I want you to sense that identity that is your own and the purposes that are yours, the joy that is a part of your being. And hold that feeling of exaltation and experience, hold it and remember it to the end of your days, and know that within you there is the road to travel whenever you will; the road to self-knowledge and to understanding.

(Somewhat softer.) And then, bringing this energy back with you to your physical frame. Let it come down and fill your physical image with joy and vitality, with energy that will fill out your cells and your tissues, with energy that will heal whatever is wrong with your physical being, with energy that will straighten out your thoughts, open up the self that you know to the knowledge that belongs to you *(loud)* and has belonged to you before the beginning of your time.

Now return to the room, open up your eyes, and feel it filled with the energy that is your own from the source that existed before the self that you now give a name, but the energy that is yours by right and the energy that sustains you.

I would do this by whispering, but it is more fun this way.

I have a secret to tell you. You can spring it on Ruburt. He is getting new glasses and new frames that are in style with the times, and he will not want me to toss them across the room like that *(tosses glasses)*. So it can be a class joke.

(Jane told her dream about Florence and Sally.)

Now, our regular members will find themselves having more group class dreams, and when you do not have group class dreams, there is a reason for it.

(To Dee G.) And I would like our friend over here, the Lady of the Initials, invited in, on these dream adventures.

(To Sheila.) And I would like to ask this little one with the red hair—I will not look at her because I frighten her—in the corner to relax; and tell her it will be all right. And do not worry about it. That is the first smile I have seen on you, and it is delightful.

Keep particular track of your dreams. You are working out reconciliations in the dream state involving your reincarnational episodes. Now your class reflects what you are doing, so always look beneath the surface, and examine your class reactions as you examine your dream reactions. All actions are valid—and I do not want to hurt anyone's feelings—but some dream actions are far more intelligent than some waking ones; and I will close Ruburt's eyes so that no one knows to whom I am speaking.

(To guests.) Now, I am glad that you came to class this evening; and all of you *(long pause)*.

(To Dee G.) There are two small doors here, and you do not need them.

([Dee G:] "Doors?")

Doors. And each one is a letter. *(Dee G. laughs.)*

Now, I bid you all a fond good evening. And watch your progress this week, in the dream state. And remember to correlate your dream activities with your waking activities. Do not make such a large division. Your experience is your own, in whichever dimension you have it.

(To Mary Ellen) I thought the light would dawn.

Now, I bid you all a fond good evening.

(To Sue.) And thank you for all your hard work.

([Sue:] "My pleasure.")

ESP CLASS SESSION, NOVEMBER 2, 1971
TUESDAY

Now I am taking these off gently so you all can see, and tell Ruburt I will not hurt his precious new glasses. Now will you take them gently from me, please?

All plants have minds. They may not have physical brains but they all have minds of their own as you would interpret it, and they are highly active. There are many more experiments that you can do, and I hope that you will, with the nature of plant activity and consciousness. It will help you all to get out of yourselves to some extent

SESSION 11/2/1971

and for the following week for regular students there is something that I want you to do, and it is this. For one week stop asking questions of the universe and simply listen to what it has to say to you. As soon as you ask questions, you are necessarily directing information in a certain manner which is all right, but for counterpoint this week simply listen.

Now the universe speaks in many voices, and it can indeed speak through a leaf if you have the wits to listen. Then you can learn much. It can speak in the silence of a room if you have the wits to realize that beneath sound there is what our friend, the physicist over here, might call antisound. That beneath the sounds that you hear there are other sounds, and I do not simply mean beneath the range of your hearing. At times you fill the atmosphere, as you think of it, with questions and with noise and you demand answers. Yet all the time far more important messages are there for you if you would once forget your questions and simply listen. Concepts that you have not thought of are there for you.

Now I have let you all play and it is good for you. It is like using your physical muscles, but beyond the playing that you are doing there are also more important issues, and you should learn of them. There should be questions in your mind besides, what was I in the previous life? How do I relate to others? How am I doing? Am I good or am I bad? Such as, what is the nature of reality?

What is the meaning of existence? I can verbalize

some answers for you, and I try to do so, but through direct experience and through opening yourselves up you will receive direct knowledge even though you may not be able to verbalize it later. And you will not get such knowledge by asking goodies of the universe like, what was I before? There is nothing wrong and much good to understand and receiving such information, but this is not all you should be concerned with. In the silence of your own thoughts, listen. As I have told you before, look where there seems to be nothing. Between sounds, between objects, not in your thoughts but between your thoughts, and there you will find answers but not to questions that you postulate in a demanding manner. And this is what I want you to do for the following week.

What does the plant say? Forget that the plant speaks to you, but what does the plant on its own say? What does the tree say? Not as you are related to the tree, but what does it say, for it speaks.

What docs the air mean when it swirls about the windows? How is this related to the nature of reality, for it is? You are focusing your questions too deeply upon yourselves and in so doing you are cutting down the kind of information that you can receive.

Now I will let Ruburt have his spectacles back, but I want to open you all up to those unspecified dimensions that escape your notice. I do not know whether you will have a class break, but you will have a Seth break. And my welcome to those of you who are new for the evening. I want to shake you out of yourselves for a change.

(To Arnold.) I want you personally to consider what I said about sounds on the other side of silence. You forgot to tell him that.

(After break.)

There are a few things I want to say before our friend closes his class.

(To Gert.) Now, first of all, over here to our profiled friend you are already the self that you want to be so do not let it bother you so. Relax more with what you are doing and let the perceptions from the whole self become your own. You are making artificial separations. You are trying too hard to be too good in other words. The self that you are is already good. The compassion itself is already there so you do not have to work so hard to be compassionate. Simply allow yourself to be.

([Gert:] "May I ask you a question?")

You may indeed.

([Gert:] "If a bull says you may go into his pasture, you may go into his pasture, but when a person wishes to heal there are three things; the physical, emotional and psychological, is that correct?")

It is indeed.

([Gert:] "Well, the physical says the bull you may come into my pasture, but you may not come in this one area and you may not touch me.")

Then that is the problem of the bull and not yours. Bulls are very contrary creatures.

Now I want you all to ease up and realize that you

are also your entities now. The deeper self wants you to become familiar with its own identity. The reincarnational material is excellent, but many of you have been overemphasizing it so that it serves to set up separations within you, and you think in terms of separate selves and this is not the case. That is why I want you to be more open this week. To listen uncritically. To not set the bands or questions of any specific nature but to listen as you go about your day. To listen to the day.

Now what I am saying sounds extremely simple, easy, and it would make very uninteresting prose but the reality that exists within my words is vital and the reality that you can experience if you follow my words is vital. As our friend over here began to experience what happens when Ruburt leaves trance, so your thoughts leave their own pattern, and your emotions impress the physical reality that you know with all kinds of effects of which you are unaware.

I want you to settle yourselves within the moment as it exists for you. Do not take it for granted. Do not take anything for granted this week, either that objects are stationery or that time goes from one moment to the next. Simply watch the experience that you have and try not to transpose old concepts upon it, but leave yourselves open for the fresh experience of what <u>is</u> now. And begin now. Your thoughts, all of your thoughts at this moment, to you seem to come and go without a trace and yet they leave traces that you do not see, nor perceive, nor even sense, and yet if you quietly examine your experience, if you listen to the universe, you can begin to perceive some of these realities and that is what I want you to do. In the dreaming state as well as the waking state.

And now I do bid you all a good evening and yes, there is a connection over there *(to Sheila)* with the man of whom you spoke earlier.

And now I bid you all a fond good evening, but we have a question from our friend over here.

([Bette:] "During break Jane stood here talking to Dee and as I stood and watched these two, Jane all of a sudden was a very little girl looking up at this man and the man was trying desperately to get Jane to say that she was sorry for something that she had done, and Jane would not say this. The conversation had absolutely nothing to do with what my thoughts or what I was picking up on these two. Was Dee like a headmaster in a school that Jane attended?")

Your perceptions were quite legitimate. Now I will end the session and leave it to our friend to end the class, but listen this week.

ESP CLASS SESSION, NOVEMBER 16, 1971
TUESDAY

(Phil had been talking about Igor.)
I took the glasses off easily.

(To Phil) You are learning to tap your life energy, to feel its power, its availability and its strength, and that is good, and do not label it. Know that the energy is there

for whatever purpose you desire to use it.

(To Mary Ellen) And in the same way over here, do not be so impatient. You are opening channels. You are clearing them out. You are opening doors to your own perception. Be content with that and do not put so many questions to the voice of the universe when it speaks, and you will get a clearer message. And do not ask for so many specifications.

([Phil:] "Seth, then is Igor an actual separate personality or am I just expressing what I pick up and relating that energy?")

You are tapping the energy of your being, the inner self, with which you have not been familiar. You are picking up information, often of which you conscious self is not aware. But it is part of your own heritage, a part of your being. And it is a first step and a good step. It is an unfolding. And if you were more natural about it, it would come more easily. It is as natural to you as the air.

Now, you have all been changing your relationships, not only because of what has gone on in class physically, but because of what you have been doing in the dream states. And as you know, in another layer of reality, this is the dream state, and in that level of reality I am telling you to remember your dreams, and I have already told you that this evening you will have a class dream session, and this is it. And in this level of reality, I am telling you that you will have a class dream session this evening, and in that other level of reality, you will remember. If you did not insist upon setting up so many divisions, you could see far more clearly. I ask you to do things *(to Gert)* in a minute I will be with you—all of you, and some of you do these things and some do not.

Now, if for a week, you looked at your present physical daily reality and your sleeping reality as not two separate existences but one, then they can merge in a most dramatic way. When I say this, you are bound to interpret my statement to mean that daily waking reality may become dreamy, or blurred or indistinct. But this is not what will occur. Both realities are your own, and the sense of division need not exist.

As you all know, you can become as conscious sleeping, and you do, as you are in the normal state, or now when you listen to me. But, if you go to bed this week each night with the idea that you are not sleeping in the terms in which you usually accept that term, but you are instead changing the focus of your consciousness and that you will be as much awake and consciousness, then you will become aware of what you do consciously when you sleep. And you can all *(to Sheila),* all succeed to some extent or another in this experiment, and anything you learn or remember, or take back with you, will be more than worth your while. I cannot impress upon you too deeply the validity of both these existences, that you consider dual.

Feel, now, your own consciousness. Look about you and see what you perceive. Listen to what you hear. Now, I tell you that in another reality you are presently sleeping, in your terms, and yet how conscious and aware you are.

Now, when you go to sleep this evening, in your terms, you are every bit as much this conscious and aware. Your consciousness is not inhibited, it is not blurred. You have simply hypnotized yourselves into the concept of unconsciousness. Now, there is no such things as unconsciousness. You simply turn your conscious feelings and perceptions and abilities into different directions. You have a consciousness, and you use it in a multitudinous fashion. In this reality you only accept it as valid when it is directed toward physical matter and perception. But through understanding, you can direct it elsewhere and become aware of this.

Now, I would like you to do this for the week, seriously and on your own. Make the effort. It is within each of your abilities to do this.

Now, I had a question over here from our friend The Rogue.

([Gert:] "On this business of the Alpha layers, this again is a changing of focus, it is not?")

It is, indeed. And all are native to you. All are native to you.

([Gert:] "Hmm. Ruburt told us last week to become aware in the dream state at the Alpha III level, and I did, and I had my tape recorder on next to me, and I gave myself the suggestion that whenever I got something, I would turn it on...")

You had better watch that machine.
([Gert:] "Why?")

That is all I will say for now.

([Gert:] "Will it start talking back to me? I've been getting stuff. You spoke to Phil about this energy form that's a kind of idealization or realization of the inner senses. Is that what I've been getting?")

That is correct. And you form your own reality.

([Gert:] "When I do this mirror trance, I'm getting an image on the wall behind me of my 'Golden Boy.' Is that a projection of my inner self?")

It is, indeed, to help you identify.

([Gert:] "In other words, this isn't an entity separate from me?")

It is your symbol...

([Gert:] "Of me...")

To make the idea clearer, you form the symbol. And its vagueness or its clarity is important to you.

([Gert:] "In other words, the Alpha I, II, III...")

I give you the numbers for your own edification. They are meaningless.

([Gert:] "It doesn't mean, say, a deeper trance?")

It does not, indeed. It means alternate focus of consciousness, in other kinds of realities that do exist within your own. But your experience in them will be highly colored by you, as your experience here is colored by you.

([Gert:] "Are you saying then that what I get on that recorder is still being distorted?")

I am saying in this physical reality you look about you en masse and you see a variety of objects upon which you all agree. But within that context, your experience is far different. Some of you find a joyful world, and some of you are pursued by evil. Your experience dictates what you make of the objects that exist as root assumptions within this reality. Now, in other realities and in the Alpha state, there are certain root assumptions like your objects, but you will perceive these again in your own individual manner, and you must learn to differentiate there as you do here. And some of you do not always learn how to differentiate. This is to you *(Sue)* in one specific instance, for there is one area in which you do not realize you are projecting. It is to everyone, but it is to you *(Sue)* in this instance.

Now, I am going to let you all take a break.

([Sue:] "The creation of individual symbols of self is what Dave Zale did in that incident, wasn't it?")

It was, indeed. I was aware of that, incidentally.

([Sue:] "Aware? At the time it happened?")

I was indeed.

([Sue:] "Uh, do you mean that in our terms you were there?")

I was aware. When any of you think of another, you are aware whether you know it or not, and when he thought of me, I was aware.

([Sue:] "Then that old man was himself?")

It was indeed. I helped him out.

You are so close, some of you, to understanding that cannot be verbalized, and yet I cannot give you a boost because they must come from you.

([Hope W:] "Seth, can you suggest what specific daily

steps I can take to develop my inner senses?")

I will let our friend Ruburt take care of that for you on Friday. He is programmed to give you that kind of information. *(Laughter.)*

(To Bette during break.) You know what I said, and you know that you know.

(After break, Bette described her feelings about her friend Jason.)

Now, all of you who come to this class, to one degree or another—to one degree or another have one thing in common—you are not afraid of the unknown. It intrigues you. You are adventurous as far as the unknown is concerned, and you are determined to seek it out and make it known. You are trying to do just that.

(To Bette.) So do not turn aside from that endeavor, and again do not judge the information that you get in the terms in which you are used to judging it. There is a validity to the information that you received, and accept that validity. Accept it, and realize that the nature of its validity will come to you. Do not insist it must necessarily mean that this is completely your imagination, or hogwash, or that it is the God's truth on the other hand, and that there is nothing but an abyss between. You have picked up legitimate information. You have perceived and to some extent had the sensations of the personality that was Dolly Madison. Your Jason tried to give you this information in the clearest way that he could. But because you insist it must be one thing or another, legitimate reincarnational information or complete fantasy,

there was no way he could give you this information clearly, except in the way that he gave it to you. So do not thrust it aside and do not blame your Jason or yourself, but be thankful for what you have, which is valid information. You have a close affinity with that personality and there were some strong connections between you and that personality, and it is for this reason that you were able to pick up the sensations and emotions so strongly. There is still, however, some conscious control and questioning on your part that inhibit the details that you receive so that they must be given in a certain fashion, and this is also understandable and a part of your progress. So do not throw out the baby with the wash water. It is clean, good water, and I see we are going to have a sphinx in class, and that is something new.

Now, I will let you return to your discussions of the week's activities.

(Gert asked Bette about her feelings toward Jason. Bette explained that while she never read very much history, Jason seemed to know a lot about it.)

... *(Words lost)* far as the inner self is concerned, for you must translate what you receive. You are more than you think you are. You are each more than you think you are. Then why should it amaze you that you are beginning to use and recognize some of the information that belongs to your entire identity? Because you give yourselves certain names does not mean that you are not one self. You are given names as children in this life, and so you give names to other portions of yourselves as they seem to become born within your psyche. And yet, this is all a portion of your own identity. It is you. It is the voice that speaks within you, whether or not you listen, the information that is a heritage of your own, that is a part of yourself, that has always been with you. It is the self that was familiar to you before you learned to speak. The messages, therefore, come, as far as class is concerned, to this time from the entire entity, the inner identity, whatever word you want to use or coin. The innermost portions of yourself that is indeed a part of all energy, must be sifted through the self that you now recognize, and your job is to learn how to receive the information and how to open and use the inner self. But these are all evidences in your own experience of the multidimensionality of your own personality. You have the evidence within you.

Now, this identity of which I speak, from which you receive your energy and your information, this identity of yours personally, is indeed infinite. It does not have bounds. It seems to you that there are divisions within it, but it is only because from your point of view, you are working upward. You are learning to open these channels to that identity, but that identity within each of you is infinite. The names you give it at its various stages, for they appear like stages to you, are relatively meaningless, except that they give you a point of reference. At times you will cut through to a more clear rate of information or perceptions than you have ever received before. At other times it will seem that you receive trivia and meaningless information. But you must persist.

Now, all of this effort, in your terms, will be quite valuable to you in this existence, as well as in others, in your terms. But the potential is within you now, and the source of your knowledge is indeed infinite. It is only you who have to learn how to draw upon it and use it. And in your terms it will seem to appear at different stages. It will seem to... get better. You will seem to draw upon a greater source as you learn to use your own abilities. And in all cases, the ego that you know develops and learns, and this alters the nature of the self that you are now, and it changes the characteristics of the ego as you presently think of it.

Now, when you change the character of the ego as you think of it, you change it not only for yourselves, but for the species of which you are a part. You are involved, therefore, in a spiritual and psychic evolution, in your terms. For the time will come when reincarnational information will be considered as you now think an instinct is. It will be a part of you. And that kind of development is growing now in groups like this throughout the world. So you work not only for yourselves, but you work for others, and you change not only yourselves, but you change others, and you alter the species of which you are a part.

In one manner of speaking, of course, the change has already occurred, and we are speaking of ancient knowledge. And that ancient knowledge is dependent upon what was done here, and in some few other groups, and in what is being done in the dream state throughout the world. You may say it has been done, for it has. But in your reality you are doing it now. So be brave.

And I bid you a fond good evening. I want you, however, to read this session, to digest it and understand it as best you can. I want you to realize the importance of what has been said, and of your own activities.

ESP CLASS SESSION, NOVEMBER 23, 1971
TUESDAY

(Class had been discussing dream realities, personality, etc., for about an hour; Gert and Sheila began talking back and forth on Sheila's ideas on separate personalities, when Jane interrupted to say that she had one impression that the "hole in the universe" had opened up in Sam Levine's house and a crowd of people were flying from it into the room. She added that she thought their teacher was standing at the table by the windows. We went into Alpha to see what we could get most of us had that impression of others in the room and Jane got the words to a chant, which she wrote down. As she started to read this chant to us, she suddenly threw her head back and wailed the words in an extremely loud voice; she then remained in trance for five minutes or so, and began to speak in a liquid, near whisper.)

Sumari
ispania
wena nefari

dena dena nefari
lona lona Sumari!

(Sumari:) It is with this always we begin, and we begin our classes. It is with this chant always that we begin our endeavors in our space. It is not your own, and only a translation, for we do not use verbal communication. It is always with the facsimile of what we have heard that we begin our work, and in many guises and in many ways you are acquainted with our activities. We have always been here, in your terms, as you have always been in other places and other times, and there is a great familiarity and wonder on our part that you are still involved in these endeavors which were begun in your terms so many centuries ago, and in ways that you cannot now presently comprehend. And yet you are even familiar with what comes out as what appears as my voice in your own traits and your own translations. There are cities that we have built that you have helped us build. There are wonders here, wonders in your own reality, that we helped build in other ages in your time. We have been here many times, and you have been where we are.

Sumari!

(The second voice which came through about twenty minutes later, was louder and sounded "older.")

(Other Sumari:) And I am Sumari in another guise. And all of you have your masks and guises that you wear and have worn. I am Sumari in another guise. And all of these guises are myself, and all of your guises are yourselves. And as I dwell in many realities, so dwell you in

many realities. You will learn to become aware of these—you are learning. I am aware of all your activities. I am aware, for example, of your Seth and of your Seth II. We are all Sumari. Now we are appearing more clearly in terms that you can understand. But we are all Sumari, and if you are all Sumari and never forget that you are all Sumari, and you have always been Sumari. It is the name of your family.

([Gert:] "Are there other family names?")

(Much later and softly.) It is the name of your family. It has always been the name of your family, and there are many families. I am telling you your family name, and you are learning of your heritage. I am Sumari. You are Sumari. Thank you for coming to our class.

ESP CLASS SESSION, DECEMBER 7, 1971
TUESDAY

(Jane played a tape of the Sumari session she and Rob had during the week. Sumari came through to explain the tape, then Seth spoke.)

You are all in at the start of something, and surely you do not want it all explained for you and written out in black and white. Save the discoveries for yourselves. I do not want to cheat you of them. I am interested as to how you will use your new Sumari experience, and how you will interpret, and how well you can read between the lines and within the words. And I will give you some clues out of the great goodness of my heart.

It is true that the Sumari do not communicate verbally, and yet so far you have been given what seems to be the rudiments of a language and why? You will know, but it is much more fun if you figure it out for yourselves. You are also being introduced, or you will be introduced, to some different kinds of concepts and to some different kinds of communication, so be on your toes. There should also be communications in one way or another in the dream state.

Now if you were not the Sumari you would not be here at this particular time, and if all of you did not know what it was to be Sumari you would not be here at all. You have been given a language it seems that is not a language. And since you have been given it there is a reason for it, and what earthly good is a language that is not a language? An ancient language that never was and within those paradoxes what meanings are there for you to learn? Now I have—I've always been Sumari. I am a tough old Sumari. I am a Sumari of the old school. A Tumali of the old school. And what is there about a language that has both beginnings and endings in it as you think of them, elements of a distant past and portents of what perhaps languages might be in your future? And why do you need a language beside the one that you have? And you need not worry, you will not have to learn declensions. I would not have you stew over that with all of your other problems *(to Bette).*

(To Natalie.) There is one element you have not thought of, you have another record keeper over here.

([Natalie:] " A squeaky one, too." [Referring to noise of the tape recorder.])

A squeaky one indeed, but a record keeper.

Now all of you to some extent in your dream work keep records, and as such you are dealing with language as you know it, and you are interpreting your experience in terms of a mundane language that is as much a deception as it is a reflection of your feelings and experiences, for you cannot find words within your language to express your own feelings and experiences. Now, are you witnesses of the beginning of a language, the birth of a language that never existed? Are you witnesses of the reemergence of a language that was never spoken? Did it ever occur to you that there are languages that have never been verbalized, that beneath the words that you know and speak there are other sounds and other meanings that you do not approximate with the language that you know? Did it ever occur to you that there are other methods of communication and ways of learning what they are and steps to learning them?

Now you are beginning to communicate backward and trying to put aside the language that you knew and the phrases that you took for granted in order to approximate a more pure communication. One way of doing this would be to take several steps away from the language that you know to get into somewhat unfamiliar territory and to learn your way there, and then to be taken further down the primrose path where little by little the vowels and syllables themselves would disappear until you are at the pure sound and beneath that with true feeling. You see but a representation of me, as you realize. You see but a representation of this Sumari, as you realize. You see but the representation of yourselves in the mirror, as you realize, but behind these representations are larger multidimensional realities, and we have many teaching methods and you are apt learners. And we will indeed, with your permission and consent, lead you into other areas where you need not rely only upon the communication that you now take for granted, and we must begin by building bridges and so we shall.

And now you may all take a Seth break except, of course, I will answer our friend here from Richelieu's time.

([Bette:] "Could we call this language a telepathic language because we are so used to sounds and physical things around us that we have to have a vehicle to connect us to other things?")

You are coming very close, and that is an excellent starter. A very good comment indeed. When you walk merrily singing we want you to feel safe. We do not want you to think that you are taking a gay step across the abyss of reality and the universe with nothing, no bridge, to hold you there. You would be frightened, indeed.

([Bette:] "And this language, if we...")

It is your rope. Now you may all take a Seth break.

SESSION 12/7/1971

(Gert remarked it was good to hear Seth speak again.)

That was a delightful statement, and I have been here all along. Someone has to overlook the goings on here. While the cat is away the mice will play and the Sumari are the trap.

Listen to what is being said, and to what is not being said. Now give us a moment and listen to what is being said and to what is not being said and remember what I just told you. Your Seth break is over. In halves you will see what I mean later. Now listen to what is said and to what is not being said.

(A short pause then Sumari came through with a message for each class member. She also explained a drawing Phil had made while listening to Jane and Rob's session.

(Class described what had been said, then Seth came through.)

Do surprises never end? In what voices and what languages do truths come and in what packages and in what forms? And what the heart knows needs no translation, and the universe does indeed speak without words and so the truths that come to you do indeed, to some extent, come packaged or you would not perceive them. And you would throw them away for you would think the air cannot speak and space makes no noise, and in the silence there is no voice and no meaning and so voice and sound and language are given you. But let you remember that the language and the sound and the noise are packages that have been parceled for you, but for you personally, tailored for you exactly according to your own purposes and needs.

If, and I am speaking now metaphorically, if-if-if-if-if there was ever a Sumari language existing in the past then it had to be created, and if you want it to be found you had better help create it. You are forming realities. There are people, there are groups of consciousness, who cannot speak. There are feelings that have no vocal expression. There are consciousness, groups of consciousness, that try to communicate and you cannot listen because you insist that they have a language.

([Gert:] "Are these the blocks of lights I get in my room?")
They are symbols and symbols are quite real.

Now if you would truly learn how to listen, and you are beginning to, then you would know what I am saying and my own speech lately is carefully calculated. In certain terms, and remembering what I told you earlier, in certain terms the Sumari language does exist, and in certain terms you know it well. The Sumaris certainly exist, and you are here because you are a Sumari. And the Sumari have a way of looking in on their own now and then and coming home. These are your own secrets I am bringing out into the open. Questions that you have within yourselves. You need ways to make the answers plain to you so that you can understand them. We work in two directions. First we try to bring interior knowledge outward into some kind of physical materialization where you can deal with it in terms of sound or vision, and then we try to get you to go inward and dispense with sound and vision, so you are always working in two directions at once. And since past, present and future exist <u>now</u> in your terms you need bridges, because you do not really understand the nature of time, so you think you need a bridge to get from past to present or from past to future or from one kind of reality to another. This is not the case, of course, but while you <u>think</u> you need the bridges they are provided, and the Sumari are voices that call to you though they do not have sound. They are memories that come to you from yourselves from both the future and the past. They are yourselves speaking to you in multitudinous voices in many languages focused for you in a particular place and a particular time. You are the Sumari who communicate with you and they are you.

Now, try to remember what I have said and try to tell our friend Ruburt when he returns. It is wearying for him to fret and wonder.

([Bette:] "I have a question that doesn't tie in with this. Will you be back?")

If you have a question then I will be here to answer it, or to fence with it, or to throw it back to you, but I will be here to do something with it.

(After break.) We had a question over here.

([Bette:] "Did you and I sit one time, a long time ago? It would be like where they served drinks.")

I would never be caught in such a location. Go ahead.

([Bette:] "And did we drink hot rum together?")

Hot rum and hot brandy. Now some evening I will give you a discourse on the benefits of hot brandy, for it was one of my favorite drinks. The rum was your idea like this concoction you brought this evening. I only like the brandy myself, and that is the answer to your question.

([Bette:] "Thank you.")

([Phil:] "May I ask a question? I met two men this week; one in the library who I felt a strong attraction for, an older man of sixty; and another one who I was greatly upset by who I met this Saturday.")

The man who upset you was much closer to you at one time than the man you were attracted to.

([Phil:] "In what way?")

He was a dear and loyal friend in another life, and you felt that he betrayed you, but he did not.

([Phil:] "What purpose did he have coming up to me in this life?")

He had no conscious purpose at all. He acted, however, as you unconsciously expected him to act.

([Gert:] "Was this friend that agitated him a priest?")

He was not a priest in a past life, he was a sailor. A gob.

Now I want you all to pay particular attention to your dreams again for some time. You should meet other Sumari in the dream state, and if you are on your toes you can discover some of the work that you do while you are sleeping and the Sumari that you meet. You can also learn more about yourselves by watching your conscious life and the Sumari that you may meet while you are waking.

(To Mary Ellen) What is your question?

SESSION 12/7/1971

([Mary Ellen:] "Not all the people that you meet in the dream state are Sumari, right? Is Dr. Winston a Sumari?")

He is indeed.

(Mary Ellen:] "I knew it. And Dr. Wilt?")

They knew each other very well. It is also your connection with Ruburt in an entirely different sequence of activity.

Now I want all of you to do two things. On the one hand be more alert and on the other hand more spontaneous. Be more alert to your spontaneous activity in other words.

(To Janice.) And do not judge yourself so harshly. I hope there is no doubt about to whom I am speaking. Treat yourself as you would a beloved friend and stop hollering at yourself all the time.

([Janice:] "I wasn't really aware that I was hollering at myself. It's just that I...")

You are criticizing yourself all of the time.

([Janice:] "Awake and asleep?")

You ride yourself too hard in that respect. Tell yourself that you are doing well and you will and you will realize it. You are doing better when you are asleep.

([Janice:] "Why can't I remember when I wake up?")

Don't worry so much about the memory. It will come to you when you stop worrying about it. Take it for granted that you can remember and you will be able to.

([Janice:] "That brings to mind the health food supplements my husband wants our family to start using. Is this necessary really?")

It does not matter whether it is necessary or not. What is the intent behind your husband's idea? Why is he suggesting it and how much harm or good will it do? Is it as important to buck his ideas because you do not agree with them or to go along and say, who knows? If he believes that the health food will help, then the health food will help.

([Janice:] "But he want us to try and talk other people into using it and to sell them. This is my criticism of myself. I can't feel it's moral to try and force it on anybody even though there's money involved and we could use the money.")

See what you think. Try the foods. If they make you nauseous do not sell them. If they can help people who believe that they can help people, then there is no harm to charge for them.

([Janice:] "But there are other ways of getting them cheaper which I feel they should get them.")

Then that is not a matter of health foods, but of honesty, and that you must deal with yourself, but tell yourself you will know the answer and make the reasons for your objections clear. Do not buck him on principle to buck him.

([Bette:] "This goes back to Sumari. Would I be right in saying that Sumari is like the very kernel or the very seed that we grow from?")

You would indeed. Carry it further.

([Bette:] "Then it's the very core from which ...when we get involved in this time and all time is going on, all our lives are going on now—past, present, future..."

(Seth singing very loudly.) Sumari is a friend of mine and their time is your time. Now I certainly hope that you have that down on tape. It may not be a melodious, but it made the point I hope.

([Bette:] "No, Seth, it did not.")

Where did we miss?

([Bette:] "Go back to the core. All these lives, all of our lives are going on now.")

They are indeed.

([Bette:] "Now if we could somehow stop everything and go back this way we would all go right back to Sumari, right? To the core?")

And you are Sumari now. The core is a core while it is more than the core. It is the seed. For example change core to seed. Sumari is the seed. It is also the tree that has grown from the seed and the leaves that have grown from the tree, and they all exist simultaneously. Did I get that across yet or did you like my song?

([Bette:] "No, I got that one."）

([Gert:] "What is espana?")

The word means forever.

([Gert:] "I got that in psy time.")

The other words in the verse that I believe you had down for forever are instead, ever, but go ahead with the elaborations of your question.

([Bette:] "All right, so we go from the seed to the tree to the leaves. Now the leaves fall off and eventually—I know that it's the same thing like I said with our lives, that all are going on at the same time. It's a cycle but does it eventually all go

back to the seed?")

The leaves, in your terms, as they fall add to further seeds. There is no difference between the leaves, the tree and the seed. These are only appearances. The seed is as much the leaf as it is the seed. It is as much the sky as it is the trunk. A tree grows as deeply within and under the earth as it does above it. It is therefore as much dirt and worms as it is bark. It is as much the birds that rest upon its branches as it is the seed that gave it birth. And in what I have said is contained the seed of your answer.

([Bette:] "I got it. Thank you.")

Now I bid you all a fond good evening.

([Janice:] "Is there any legitimacy to the information we received on the Ouija board at my grandmother's on Sunday?")

There is some, but do not misinterpret or overinterpret and do not insist too much upon specifics.

([Janice:] "Should we just forget the whole thing or should we search further?")

You can always continue. Do not limit yourself, however, by insisting upon specifics at your particular point in the game. Do you follow me?

([Janice:] "No, I'm afraid not.")

When you get the session, read what I have said and it will come to you. Give yourself greater freedom with it.

([Janice:] "We only have three weeks to make up our minds.")

So that each board session is not so critical. You should not be dependent upon the board for your answer.

You should allow the answer to spontaneously come from within, otherwise the board becomes a symbol in this particular case now alone, so that you demand the answer of it and that is not how to go about it. Does that make it clear?

([Janice:] "Yes. Thank you.")

Now I bid you all a fond good evening, and I hope you meet many Sumari in your sleep and hopefully in the waking state and I hope that you read this session well, for when you see the words written down you will also <u>hear</u> what is between the words and hidden within the vowels and syllables.

ESP CLASS SESSION, DECEMBER 14, 1971
TUESDAY

(Rob read their session of the previous evening when Seth gave more information on Sumari. Seth came through.)

You were right when you said that we are getting into more meaningful material and so I would like you all to listen so I do not have to give it twice. You are getting into some material where we compare cordellas and alphabets and that material will also tell you why we are interested in using this language at all.

([Rob:] "Thank you, Seth.")

Any time at all. Welcome to our class. We will show you what unstructured means.

([Rob:] "Can I ask a question or is it too late?")

You may indeed. It is never too late for you to ask a question.

([Rob:] "Thank you. Why was Ruburt speaking Sumari in his sleep last night?")

He has to get an education sometime. When he speaks in his sleep in Sumari, you have to learn it in order to understand what he is saying.

([Rob:] "I was going to say I couldn't even eavesdrop.")

You had better get going then.

(Rob continued reading the session.)

Wait for a moment and see how much of that they have gotten through their heads and then read the rest.

(A short discussion and then Rob continued.)

Now you can all verbalize better in the language you know than you are doing right now, and it is good for you to put what you know into verbalized terms, so I will be around here. Use the language that you have even while you are learning a new one. And again to our friend in the corner *(Bette)* you will not have to learn declensions.

(Sumari came through and gave a message to the class.)

Stay where you are. Relate to the person before whom you stand. Start to make sounds and let yourselves go along with the sounds. Look each other in the eye, let your feelings rise and then express them in the sounds that come to you. If the Sumari chant then go ahead with your own communication for the chant is to serve another purpose. Now let yourselves go freely. I am here to see what you are doing and how you are doing. Allow yourselves that freedom, all of you, you need it. And there are things that you want to say to each other that need saying.

(Seth came through again after the exercise.)

You have allowed yourselves some small freedoms this evening. There will be many ways that you will learn to use your inner senses and methods that you are finally ready to use. The Sumari language is one of these. Again in your dreams, if you are quick enough to catch them, *(to Janice)* you will find some surprises and also over here *(to Gert)* and in your feelings, not intellectualized feelings, but in your feelings in the relationships set up this evening with the three of you, there are some hints for you, so see that you discover what they are. You will be surprised and delighted when you do. Now there are surprises in store for all of you including you *(to Rob)* and this one here *(to Sue)*.

I bid you all good evening and you should be a lot smarter next week than you are this evening for there should be some interesting Sumari dialogue going on in your dreams. Now do not, and this is for you over there *(student)* and you over there *(another student)* do not, in Ruburt's terms, get hung up over what words mean. Follow along with the feelings of the sounds for that is what is important. The meanings will come through clearly and of themselves.

([Bette:] "This doesn't follow along with what you have been saying, but you have given some people what you call their whole name, like Jane is Ruburt and Rob is Joseph, what is my whole name?")

Your whole name, in those terms, is Varnelldi.

([Rob:] "How about everyone's name?")

Which language do you want it in?

([Rob:] "English.")

You want entities of pure English blood in other words. Give us a moment. Only out of the great goodness of my heart...

(Seth gives the following list of whole names.)
(Janice) Rendo
(Sue) Oranda
(Pete) Purto
(Natalie) Grendah
(Gert) Meor
(Florence) Femtori
(Sally) Shelva
(Phil) Igor

([Rob:] "I have meant to ask that for some time.")

They will thank you for coming to class this evening.

Now, the Sumari do exist and you are Sumari. Some night you may meet many more Sumari here. In the meantime be aware of the waking and sleeping and remember that *(very loudly)* the energy that sweeps through this form sweeps also through your own. And that the energy you see displayed is also available to you. Use it and delight in it. It is the foundation of your life.

And I bid you all now a fond good evening in the softest of voices.

ESP CLASS SESSION, DECEMBER 21, 1971
TUESDAY

(Sue was fumbling with the tape recorder while Jane held the reel with her finger, when Seth came through.)
She is going to grow up to be a mechanical genius.
([Sue:] "Wait! You let the tape go!")
I never pretended to be a mechanical genius.
(We discussed the Sumari "language" and what it could mean.)
Now!
([Sue:] "Wait!" [turns on Jane's recorder].)
Is it all right for me to speak now? I am waiting for your assent.
([Sue:] "Okay, go ahead..."
(Very slow, deliberate and precise, each word emphasized as though being handed to us individually, syllable by syllable:)
Each of you receive revelations every moment of your lives. Your life is a revelation. We are trying to lead you gently so that you will accept the revelations of your peers. Within you are answers and questions. The questions are to lead you to your own answers and the answers will not be the same. Each of you will read the answers in your own way.

The revelations have come through the centuries. The revelations <u>are</u> the centuries. The centuries are transparent. You can look through this history that you know. The selves that sit there know other selves. There are revelations within you that do not need words. They need to rise up like new planets into your own consciousness, and you need to treat them gently and not give them labels or names. So we are leading you away from labels and names, and for awhile you may feel confused or lonely, for you only feel safe when you can name an experience. And you want to know, what is it? What is its name? Is this language a truth? Did it exist in the past, what is it? before you would consider using it.

We want to do away with the normal punctuation of your experience, for you put periods and question marks and dashes where they do not belong. What Ruburt said earlier concerning the songs of the Sumari is indeed true. The words are stepping stones to lead you into other areas of experience. *(To Gert.)* Do not be afraid to step off of the words.

Do not think first, "Is this a true word?" Use the word as a launching pad to experience. Within the word is a wordless knowledge. Now you need the sounds to remind you. In time—in your time—you will dispense even with the sounds. You will be walking backward, in your terms, into the heart of perception. Therefore, you will leave behind many of the truths that are now familiar to you, the words that you take for granted. For when you consider an experience, you apply words to it much more than feelings: "Does this word apply, or does that word apply, or what is it; and without its label, dare I experience this unknown?"

Illuminating the centuries and the landscapes of

your thought, revelations have indeed appeared and appear now. The Bible is but one aspect, and highly distorted, of revelations that occurred, in your terms, in the past. But revelations are always, they do not end. There is not a revelation that stopped happening centuries ago. You are revelations. You are each revelations. You very carefully examine your experience. Is this valid? Is this true? but you are yourselves experiences. Are you valid? Are you true?

What is your experience at any given time without reliance upon words and labels? Where are you? What are you? What is where? Where is who? Again, Ruburt was quite correct. We want to scramble up your perceptions, so that you can experience experience and not place curtains of labels between you and your own feelings and own knowledge.

As I speak now, the revelations that you are burst into activity, and certainly you should know of this. While you think, "I am man, a member of a certain species, inhabiting a planet named Earth in this space and in this time," then you place artificial barriers between you and your perceptions. And you dwell in a world in which words grow into a distorted lens that denies your own vision. Therefore, to some extent, we will crumble the words up, crumble the words up and distort them until it seems that in the language that we use you perceive certain familiar sounds. Your associative processes find a certain feeling of safety and familiarity, leaping upon this vowel and this syllable. All delightful trickery. But a trickery that is in its own way as truthful as revelations that you are.

Now, I am using words in a different way this evening and for my own purposes. And I hope when I am finished, you will be sufficiently unscrambled to know what I am telling you, because when you are not scrambled, you do not understand what I am saying! If you possibly remember what I said last week, then we will have you dancing through your cordellas, throwing alphabets out of the window to flutter in the wind. Eat your words and see what happens.

Now you may have a Seth break, and I leave it to you to explain so sensibly to Ruburt what I have said. Unscramble yourselves, be thoroughly scrambled, and you will untopsy-turvy and know what you feel. And to scramble you further, give us a moment.

(Sumari spoke to class for some time, individually and collectively, using chants and particular characterizations. Jane then came out of trance and instructed the students to stand in various areas of the room, in answer to significant feelings she had about these positions. After meeting Florence in the center of the room, Sue wrote a short verse about their encounter and read it to class.)

(To Sue.) Now you are learning to speak Sumari; and all of you in your own way can use it, and it does not depend upon verbal understanding. It is simplicity. It is the language beneath touch, and you do not need words for it though you must translate your experience somehow. But you can do that by jangling the words that you

know and unlearning what you think you know.

I do not sing *(laughter)*.

(At break Pete described the class experience in some very Sumari English.)

Right on! *(Laughter.)*

([Phil:] "What?!")

(Very loud.) Right on! That shows you how modern and up-to-date I am, and proves that I am not archaic.

(Break. Derek presented an idea about cordellas.

(To Derek.) You are on to a clue, but you made an error. They are related. Now carry on from there.

(Here Jane came out of trance and indicated that Florence was "supposed to do something" tonight. After a few minutes, Florence drew a geometric design on a notepad and explained that she had been doodling this for years, and that it seemed important to all of us. Thereupon, with Sumari's help, class got up and walked around in a circle, all of us chanting along with the Sumari, who indicated to several of us to do certain motions. When it was over, we all sat down and Florence remarked that she felt she still hadn't done what she was "supposed" to do with the symbol.

(To Florence.) You were supposed to display it proudly and to take your place and to pass the symbol onto others.

([Florence:] "I had the feeling I should have done that, but I couldn't.")

You will be able to. The Sumari wear many guises and they... *(words lost)*.

Now, I will let you continue with your discussion.

And I will wait while you bring your feelings up into the open.

(To Pete.) Right off is much better than right on. *(Laughter.)*

NOTES FROM ESP CLASS SESSION, DECEMBER 21, 1971

During ESP Class the Sumari, through Jane, told Florence to go look out the middle window, and Sue to look at the door which they did. At the same time Florence and Sue turned and walked toward each other and met in the center of the room. Florence knelt before Sue, and Sue was stunned—for a second. Then Sue put her hand on Florence's head, and Florence got up and they embraced, and it was over.... Then Sue got the following as a concept in both Sumari and English at once.

> *I look at that which is closed.*
> *She looks at that which is open.*
> *When we meet, who has the greater power?*
> *The open is before her, but facile.*
> *The closed is stubborn, but I am strong.*
> *She kneels to the closed, but I am awed.*
> *The open has her joy in easy paces.*

ESP CLASS SESSION, DECEMBER 28, 1971
TUESDAY

(Following a discussion of Sumari, Lawrence Briggs remarked how old we all must be.)

Now I bid you good evening, and when you realize that you have been many people and that you are many people, then you will realize that you need not think so in terms of age, for you are as much now the young woman that you were back in Naples in the 14th century as the man that you now think you are, and you are not bounded by what you think of as your present age. When you realize that your own personality is indeed multidimensional, then you will realize that your age is a reality that you are presently experiencing, among many other realities. It gives you a certain viewpoint and a certain framework from which to view reality, but it is not the only viewpoint that you have available to you, and it is not the only framework from which your reality springs.

(To Sue.) Now you were quite correct, and if you will forgive me, you are in this room now all Sumari.

(To Ron.) And this applies even to you who feel that you have so many webs in front of your brain that you cannot possibly see through them, and of course you can, and the webs are there because you want to play with them at this time, and so feel free to do so. It is the viewpoint of reality that you have presently adapted, and as such it is purposely not only valid but important to you.

You have adapted it for a reason. From your particular viewpoint at this moment you will learn certain things that you think you could learn in no other way. You are like our friend over here *(Phil)* nine months ago.

But you are all Sumari despite your ages; despite your sexes; despite the fact that you think you dwell in bodies that are your own and that mean you, for your bodies, of course, cannot hold what you are.

Now two of you are particularly Sumari. Two of you over here in the corner here *(Ron and Laurie)* have still to learn that you are Sumari, but it does not matter whether you accept the fact that you are Sumari or not, because you are. And the term Sumari does not matter. It is a word that we have coined for a state of being and you can use any term that you prefer.

(To Chet.) Over here, however, is what seems to be a young gentleman from a strange town who is attending class for the first time. Unconsciously he has always been aware that he was a Sumari.

(To Jeannette.) And you have been aware that you are a Sumari.

(To Lawrence) And so have you.

There were others who were supposed to come to class tonight from afar who did not come, and they did not come because they were not Sumari. It does not mean that free will does not operate, it simply means that they knew the way and the time was not right. And you would all do much better if you did not question the definition of Sumari, for the Sumari themselves are not structured.

You are not supposed to come up with a logical definition of what Sumari is or what you are doing.

(To Bette.) And for our friend over here, Richelieu's cousin, neither are you supposed to know what each word of Sumari language means. You are to use the words again as stepping stones and that is all. At some time you no longer need them.

([Gert] "Is that what I've been getting in my dreams, at the end of a dream?")

It is, indeed.

(To Mark.) Now spontaneity knows its own order. It does not need order put upon it from the outside. Some of you fear that spontaneity is destructive. You wonder where it will lead you, but the earth as you know it is spontaneous and you can trust it, and therefore you can also trust the spontaneity of your own nature.

(To Ron.) And so you can go along with your own feelings and trust them. If you trust them, they will lead you to further feelings. When you distrust them then you become buried beneath an avalanche of unrecognized feelings that will not free you.

Now I will tell you briefly that you were involved with last week although I have already told Ruburt and Joseph in their session. You realize that nothing happens in this class that you do not want to happen. That no impetus arises that does not come from you. I do not say, "Aha, my friends need to know this and so I will stuff it down their throats." The impetus comes from you and therefore what happened last week came from you. You were indeed involved in a variation of an ancient ceremony in which you were all, in your terms, at one time involved. This was your translation of it in terms that you can understand. As what you are now is a translation of yourself in terms that you can understand. I made some comments last week. You do not have them now, but you will have them shortly for the session is not yet typed, but that will help clear up some of the questions that you have in your mind.

But remember, all of you, that your reality is structured not in logical terms as you think of logic, but that your most chaotic dream, our redhead over here *(Sheila)*, the most important symbolic episode and experiences that you have that seem so unstructured to you, and you do not understand them; that these have their own inner structure that is intuitive and you understand that structure very well whether or not you consciously admit that recognition.

Now you can all have a Seth break.

(To Pete.) And I appreciate over here, as Ruburt did, your bringing together the concepts of the Sumari cordella and the EE *(electromagnetic energy)* units. It is a very good intuitive connection.

([Bette:] "You just said something about ancient. Will you define what you mean by ancient? One time in class you said something about what we were doing was ancient now.")

Indeed, and yet newly created.

([Bette:] "Now when you talk about ancient tonight are you talking about before consciousness, like the physical reality

SESSION 12/28/1971

that we are now? Is this the ancient that you are referring to or are you talking about ancient time as we know ancient time?")

Not as you know ancient time.

(To Sue.) Did we have a question from the blue couch?

([Sue:] "This just refers to some dreams I've had, this circle ceremony. Does it somehow connect me with John Washburn?")

It does indeed.

([Sue:] "Should I try to explain this to Leon?")

I would not at this time.

([Sue:] "I would like to ask in what way this connection?...")

I will tell you at another time when you are not involved in class. Some goodies are private as far as all of you are concerned and you would not want them bandied about. That remark is to show you my great sense of modesty and how well I fit into a group.

Now I will let you take a Seth break but remember whether you have been here many times or whether you are here for the evening, you are Sumari.

(Bette remarked she gets more confused every week.)

Our friend over here plays a game. It is called "I see nothing, I hear nothing and I know nothing," but in it she goes her way and does her thing and has her Jason. She has some characteristics like our friend Ruburt. She protesteth too much. Now you may continue with your break.

(During break a discussion of the above. Lawrence remarked there is no age because there is no time.)

Now the old man, in your terms, that will be, the personal old man that you will be, exists now as the child, in your terms, that you were exists now. You can choose any perspective that you want from which to view the reality that you know. You can choose, therefore, to view the reality that you know from a self, in your terms, that you have been. There is, as I hope all of our regular students know, no past, present and future. Therefore, in your terms, the selves that you were and the selves that you will be exist now. You have only to open your focus of attention and they will become apparent to you.

(To Chet.) You will not lose the self that you are by realizing that you are other selves also. The self that you are will not desert you.

Now I want you to do something if you wish. If you do not wish, then you can sit and observe. Now I want you simply to follow along, to listen to the sounds, to let whatever images come into your mind come. Do not attempt to translate the words that you hear into words that you know. Do not get hung up on semantics. Do not get hung up on personality. In other words, simply accept an experience. Let yourselves go with it, whatever happens. If you feel like setting up barriers, then set up barriers. If you feel like letting barriers go then let them go, but do whatever you feel like doing and whatever you feel like doing, do. If you feel like getting up and standing in front of someone else and relating with them, do it. If you feel like singing, sing. If you see images, enjoy them. If your muscles cramp, then sit and feel them cramp. If you feel like examining what is going on, then examine what is going on. If you feel like joining in with what is going on, then join in. So feel free, in other words, to do whatever you feel like doing. Now give us a moment.

(Sumari came through. Some kept looking to Jane for instructions when Seth came through.)

Now remember what we are trying and simply respond as you feel and do not question and do not intellectualize.

(Sumari came through again, and then Seth.)

See how you stop to see what you are supposed to do, and how difficult you find it to relate to another person, and how you stop immediately for directions rather than relating directly to the person. How many of you, for example, find yourselves setting up blocks to the emotional feelings that come about as a result of the chanting, and yet how many of you find a response within yourselves to the chanting, for you are doing the chanting as well as Ruburt or Sumari is.

How do you think the atoms and molecules in the room are being changed and charged as a result of the sounds? How do you think the EE units are being changed and charged as a result of the sounds? How do you think, biologically and psychologically, you are changed by the sounds? And again the sounds come from you as well as from their seeming source.

(Lawrence said he had the feeling that it was right for him to be there.)

You feel it is right because you know that you are

old and young, male and female, physical and nonphysical, because you know that you exist in your body and outside of your body and in many bodies. You know that you have a communion with the goats that you tend. You know that when you milk the goats, to some extent you partake of the universe of which you are part. You know that the milking is in itself a sacrifice. You know that the milk becomes a part of your tissues and blood and that you will, in your turn, return back to the earth and that the goats understand this intuitively, and that is why you understand what is happening in this room. But what is happening in this room happens all the time unconsciously within all of you.

Now all of you try again not to try. Right off is better than right on, so try not to try. Try, in other words, to feel what you want to do at a given time. To give you a sense of freedom, if you do not want to do anything, do not do anything, and the others should not be offended. A sense of privacy is always respected here, but also realize the sacred nature of spontaneity and of your own feelings, and do not make logical deductions now. You can make logical deductions when you discuss what happened, and you can be as critical as you want to be.

In the meantime, trust your sense and your feelings. Listen to what your body wants to do. Listen to what your mind and your feelings want to do. Do not look to whoever is speaking for directions, but follow through. If you do not feel like doing what seems to be suggested, do not do it. If you feel, however, as if you would like to do it, but do not have the guts to do it, then trust yourself and go ahead. If instructions seem to be given, follow them if you want to. If you feel like standing and looking out the window and turning your back to the whole thing, then do it, but at least know what your feelings are.

(After the Sumari experience, Seth came through.)

(To Jeannette.) You did very well and we chose you because we knew you would break the ice. You are a good icebreaker.

(To Chet.) There is a connection with our friend over here and Nebene.

(To Ron.) And webs are beautiful things.

(To Laurie.) And so are people that (*words lost*) of others.

Now give us a moment.

(Sumari came through and connected Lawrence, Ron and Mark. Then Seth came through.)

Now in the 14th century in what is now called Spain there was a family unit and this was the father *(Lawrence)* and this was the wife *(Ron)* and this was the child *(Mark)* and they have met, in your terms, after many years. Now I think that you should all celebrate their family reunion. You can celebrate with a drink or a Mu, and I suggest that you celebrate with a grand Mu, those of you who know what a Mu is. I do not sing and I do not Mu, so we will let Ruburt sing and Mu.

(The class did a Mu then Sumari came through with another message for the family, then Seth came through again.)

Now, you have all been involved in an experiment, and I hope that you all profited. I want you to go over your feelings and your reactions. I want you to accept them and question them, there is no difference and that is what you must understand.

I bid you all then a hearty good evening, but all of you will be working while you sleep. And I hope you all keep tabs so that you are aware of your dream activities. And I hope you realize what you have done this evening, and as Ruburt seems to you to be many people so are you, in your terms, many people. And he simply shows those portions of his reality that are also counterparts of your own reality that exists within you. If this personality is multidimensional then so are your own. *(Very loudly.)* And so I bid you all a fond good evening, and again, I let you know that the vitality that sings through this form sings also through your own.

([Gert] "Were you here to the end of the class last week?")
I was indeed.
([Gert:] "Was I too far afield?")
I said, if you remember, that the bull's problems to some extent were also his own, but I will have something to say to you about what occurred last week at a later date in class. In fact to both of you.

([Chet:] "Is there any connection between the two of us [Mark and himself]?")
You left your family group. He left his family group before you. You were a female then. He was a male and you were not approved of, and so he told them to go to

hell. By now you should know that it meant no difference what you told him.

I bid you all now a fond good evening and I ask you to be adventurous, to be spontaneous, to follow the ways of your own consciousness. I cannot follow the ways of your own consciousness. Only you can travel that route, for there is no other consciousness like your own, and no one can understand the truths as you can understand them, and in understanding them you create new truths. Truths are not done and finished. They are new like the flowers that eternally grow.

ESP CLASS SESSION, JANUARY 4, 1972
TUESDAY

(During class Jane showed what Rob got in Sumari and her translation of it.)

Now the Sumari are gathering together and the Sumari are coming home and you should be prepared for some emotional reunions for they will come from near and afar. And in your dreams, those of you who are able to remember, you will be given instructions as to how to greet them, as to how to use the language without learning declensions.

What Ruburt received with his numbers, and through his friend Nabene, is only a beginning and more, indeed, will be given.

(To Arnold) And some information that will be partic-

ularly of interest to you in terms of concepts and I thoroughly expect you to rise to the bait.

Concepts, however, must be put into living knowledge and into practice or they are not meaningful and so the concepts that are received will also be translated in such a way that you can use them and put them into daily practice so you will at sometime be able to speak your body with more effectiveness than you do now.

The Sumari are coming home and they come regardless of age or sex in your terms and there are meeting places in many areas of the world to which they will travel beside here. I expect, however, all of you to be interested in two things. In concepts, I want you to play with them, go along with them, see where they lead you. And in practice in making concepts flesh in using them. Now see what you can do, play with what you can do. Do not strain to understand what will be said or sung. Simply go along with it and see what images or feelings or concepts it brings out in you.

Now give us a moment so our dear friend here *(Sue)* can turn on the mechanical gadget and get it right and make sure that all the zeros are where they are supposed to be. We must protect the integrity of the zero also you know. Now give us a moment and remember do not strain. Let yourselves go and follow the sounds.

Sumari came through with a song then Seth spoke.

Let us see how far you are able to follow and where the sounds lead you and where you were lead by what was within the sounds, for the sounds are a cordella and I am a Sumari cordella. This evening the sounds had many meanings and they were to be deciphered by each of you personally. Some of you were to be reminded of events and images that were extrememly important in your lives and that have connections with other lives and such was the memory that came into your mind.

(To Bette) Now there is some information that you are afraid of, our dear cousin of Richelieu, and the charge is on your end only and it is harmless. It is only important because you have cherished it so as one can cherish a great pain and be afraid of letting it go and think "this pain sets me apart" and all you have to do is let go of it. Now the antagonism that you sense is your own projected outward and our Mary Ellen here who is very close to you psychically, picks it up, receives it and magnifies it so you are no help. It will be of great benefit to you in fact, to face the entire issue for it will make your relationship with one of your children in particular much easier when you do. There are hangovers in other words, that can be easily dispensed with. And I tell you that out of the great goodness of my invisible heart.

([Bette:]) "Thank you, Seth."

Anytime, right off, I learn too, you see.

(Richard Kendall felt he was given a gift.)

Now each of you are indeed being given a gift each time the Sumari sings or speaks and it is up to you to decipher that gift. In one way Ruburt was correct, it is a gift from the universe but it is also a gift from yourselves. From the inner self and it is up to you to be free enough to understand this and use it. Beside that there are significances in the vowels and syllables and sounds that will be explained to you as you learn what they are through experience. You are to use your inner senses while you are in this room therefore. You are to use your own perceptions. Be aware of your feelings and interpret them. The vowels and syllables do affect you differently, not only as a group, but individually, and they are meant to. To the extent that you understand this, you will be able to utilize much of this material for your own benefit. And at home and in your dreams and in healing and in maintaining the effectiveness and integrity of your own physical image. Now I am going to pause and I expect a different translation of this in English to our friend Ruburt before we proceed, and proceed we will.

(To Bette) Now we will not proceed with you any further unless you are willing, so rest assured. When you say you are willing we will proceed and until that point we will not, so you can feel safe and come to your own decision. Even I would not push a cousin of Richelieu. Let it be said that I know my place.

(During break Sally remarked we would be reminded of the past.)

And some of you will be reminded of the future in your terms. And I had something to say to him over here too and you did not record it. *(Meaning Lawrence Briggs.)*

([Student:] "That had something to do with....")

The magic word.

(After break Bette asked why Phil was on trial. Sumari came through with an experience involving Phil, who was on trial, Pete K., and Jed Martz as witnesses, Richard as the judge

and Natalie as the scribe. At the end of the experience all involved formed a circle and joined Sumari in a chant.

(When this was finished Seth came through and said:)
Let that be a lesson to you.

ESP CLASS SESSION JANUARY 11, 1972
TUESDAY

(During class a discussion of reincarnation, space and time. Jane read more of her translation of Rob's Sumari statement. Sumari came through with a message to Bette and Sue. After a discussion of that, Valerie described a dream in which a face appeared, then Seth came through.)

Now the powers were your own and the face that you saw was a materialization of your own angers because you are not using your full abilities and so it was one part of the self, angry, yelling at another portion. Also, you knew very well that the Sumari were coming home and so you approximated in your own terms the sound of the Sumari as it presently exists. It is an impressionistic language.

([Valerie:] "But later when it spoke to me it didn't seem to be speaking like that.")

You, in your dreams, have many, many purposes. The main point of the dream, however, was that a portion of you was reminding you of abilities that you had. Now at one time you misused them, but they are yours nevertheless and now you are not using them to their full extent.

([Valerie:] "At the end, why did it turn away?")

You turned away. You turned away from yourself both

from the anger and from the implication of the abilities.

([Valerie:] "Who was the friend?")

You know who the friend is. It will come to you. Now she wears another face, as you all wear other faces.

Now your are barely beginning. At one time, bear with me, *(long pause)* there was what we may call a federation of consciousness, though that is not the best term. But consciously a group of people upon this earth managed to remember old truths. They remembered that they formed physical reality from the vitality of their own thoughts and fellings and images. They knew how to do this consciously. They knew how to speak the body. They knew how to speak the wind. They knew how to send their thoughts and feelings out into a universe and to make the kind of universe that they wanted. Many times the knowledge has been forgotten and many times it has been reclaimed and so hopefully you will reclaim it once again.

There are methods that you barely understand by which you give your bodies vitality and strength. There are ways and methods by which you daily send forth your image out into the universe. There are ways and methods by which you form each organism within you and those organisms that you perceive as outside of you. Hopefully you will reclaim these methods consciously and use them. This is the endeavor that we are presently engaged in. It will lead us into the heart of perception as you understand it and as you do not, as yet, understand it. It will lead you into the understanding that your hopes, as you think of them in the present, exist not only in what you think of as the present, but in the past and future as well. That you form the universe as you know it en masse and individually from the focal point of this moment, from the focus of this moment that all of your selves exist now and are not done and finished anymore than you are done and finished. *(Very loudly)* And anymore than I am done and finished. Anymore than my reality is no more than it appears to you in this room, for your reality is far more than it seems to be to you as you sit within this room. En masse and individually, as you know, you form the room, the funiture, the time, the setting in which it now seems to you, you exist. It seems to you that there is no other existence for you personally but this room and this time and this moment and yet, of course, you create it. You create the selves, who in turn create the images that you know. Within you this knowledge is apparent and speaks to you if you would listen. You think that there is somthing very esoteric, mysterious and strange often in what I say and there is not. What I say is as intimate to you as your own breath is if you would but feel your breath. If you would but once give up the defenses that you have set between what you think of as your intellect and what you think of as the rest of the self.

Now the sounds and the chanting of the Sumari as you presently understand it, has many purpose. There are physical repercussions in your own bodies that occur if you would but listen to your bodies and feel them when the songs go on, for there is language beneath words. Meanings in sounds that your atoms and molecules understand and react to and dance to and combinations that are there for you to open individually.

Where, from without, can truths come to you? They must come from within you. I can only encourage you to open yourselves to them, to listen; to be, to experience your own being. Not to experience your being second-handed through the experience of others or through the opinions of others, but through your own experience and so I hopefully expect that you will learn these methods as you get them here and as you receive them for yourselves in your own ways. After all this time you still do not personally accept the fact that you are, in your terms at this moment, the sum of your own thoughts and emotions about yourselves and that whatever you want to fix you can fix, and that whatever you want to change you can change. If you do not change it is because you do not want to change badly enough. No results are forced upon you from the outside. You form the outside.

(Following a discussion of the above Seth came through again.)

Now over a period of time you will all be given a series of sounds or a particular song or chant that will be yours alone and meant to apply to you alone. I suggest that you learn the sounds and say them to yourselves all alone. They may or may not make conscious sense to you. They may or may not sound like you to you, but I suggest that you pay attention to them and that you use them. I will tell you their benefits and meanings as you learn what they are, for I would like the knowledge to come from you. And if you give me a moment we will begin with one and you will always be told ahead of time if the song applies to you. I will not do the singing, it is not in my line.

(Sumari came through with a chant for Gert—then discussion, then a chant for Arnold. Someone mentions that Seth would not sing)

I never could carry a tune.

([Arnold:] "That's a negative attitude.")

It is indeed, but I never was able to do so and at one time when I was pope I used to try very hard, and it always sounded terrible and even the altar boys drowned me out. *(Seth sang)* I could not do it and they would titter and laugh behind my back.

(Sumari gave a chant to Pete, Faith Briggs, Bette, and Valerie.

(Following a discussion of each chant, Seth came through.)

The meaning will become apparent as you become aware of the melodies and vocalize them for yourselves. They are extrememly personal and tailored uniquely for you and that is all I will tell you at this time. I will also tell you that they will have a healing quality. I will keep other goodies for later.

ESP CLASS SESSION, JANUARY 18, 1972
TUESDAY

Now let our guardian of the portals over there close the door and this time, once again, listen to the chanting and I will not give you any instructions. Do with it what you will. Use it for whatever purposes you will but be open to it. Now give us a moment. I feel quite uncharacteristic for a change with Ruburt in his skirt and this *(meaning Jane's long bangs).*

([Sue:] "I'll cut it for you.")

I may have you do that. Give us a moment, however.

(Sumari came through with a message to Molly, Pete, Bette, Phil, and Florence.

(Following a discussion of the above, Sumari came through with a message to Janice, Lawrence and Faith, then to Lawrence, Faith and Natalie.

(During a discussion of this Lawrence said he did not get the whole connection with Faith and Natalie.)

Now you were two brothers, you and your wife and you were herding animals and you were also hunting them. Now that was one sequence. In the other sequence you were a woman and our friend over here *(Natalie)* was a very unfaithful suitor and you bleieved him implicitly and he left you, as the saying goes, in the lurch. You came back however with your former brother in a wife-husband relationship and the farm connection in your later life has to do with this earlier reincarnational existence, in your terms, in which you *(Faith)* were very closely involved. And you are also getting back at our friend over here by coming as a couple to class while she now comes alone.

(After break.)

This time I want you to listen and I want you to close your eyes and to experience what you feel. Simply allow

yourself to go along with the sounds and not fight them.
(Sumari came through with a chant for class.)

ESP CLASS SESSION, JANUARY 25, 1972
TUESDAY

(During class it was mentioned that certain members who hadn't been coming regularly were back. Bette said that some members got more information than others did.)

The Sumari always come home. They have never left home and they know where home is and none of you have left your home and the Sumarian in you knows that very well.

(To Bette) Now I do not play favorites and you know that very well and when you need help you get it and when others need help they get it.

([Bette:] "Yes, but I think I was set up for that. After I said that this one [Mary Ellen] told me something that she has been thinking all week and all I did was mouth her words for her again.")

I did not say you were not set up. I just said I do not play favorites. Now you knew what you were supposed to do last week and it took you a good two hours to do it and now you want a medal.

([Bette:] "No, I don't want a medal. I would just like to know why I did it because I don't know why I did it.")

Then you should ask yourself why you did it. And if you quit telling yourself that you do not know why you did it, then you would know what you already knew, why you did it.

([Bette:] "And you aren't going to tell me why I did it, are you?")

You tell me why you did it, I am not used to such goings on. Why did you do it?

([Bette:] "I don't know.")

It was a lovely benediction. Why can't you leave it at that?

([Bette:] "Alright, I won't with you, Seth. I'll drop it if you say....)

You never drop anything. It would not be nearly as much fun if you did, for I am not reprimanding you.

Some Sumari come home quicker than others and some Sumari take their time. Some Sumari, and as you can all see I am closing Ruburt's eyes so I am sure no one knows to whom I am speaking, do they Joseph? Some Sumari play games. They are lovely games, but they are games. But there is always an opening door when the Sumari come home. Now I do not want to tell you all the answers to the Sumari development, for some of the answers you are to find out for yourselves and some of the answers cannot happen unless you discover them for yourselves. Now that is an important symbol, and were our friend here writing it down in the book I would say underline, for our book is full of such directions as underline, put that in quotes, and semi-colon.

(A pause while Rob answered the door.)

I would leave an envelope, but no one would put anything into it except questions and I have plenty of those. Now who else do you know, except those two people *(Jane and Rob)*, who would sit for one solid hour conversing in a language they do not understand? And yet you see they understand very well, and again, it is a game, for he pretends that he does not know what he knows. And all of you have only to relax and let yourselves realize what you know and follow the Sumari development when our friends here are not physically with you. And on their return I will answer your questions and I will have some of my own and I will keep you good and busy.

([Bette:] "If I don't ask you any, will you not ask me any?

I am not making any such bargains and you are not in a position to bargain either.

Now this time, if it is not asking too much, listen to the sounds that you will hear without questioning, accept them as you do the paintings and the walls and the lights and the other people in the room as things that are and perceive them in your own way, but let them come to you as the lights come to you. Otherwise I will have you learn declensions and then there will be some stink indeed from that corner over there.

(Sumari came through with a chant for class then a message to Rob and Sue, then to Rob, Sue and Bette. Following a discussion of the last part Seth came through.)

What did you do with the first part of the Sumari chant that was to all of you? You did not even tell Ruburt that that went on, so let's see to it that someone tells him and then how far along with it you were able to go and I think we should start with our fine late Sumarian over there in the corner *(to Rachel)*.

(Arnold told of a repeated scene he has had.)

You will see more and more and your vision will enlarge as you go on.

And the Sumari chants are to lead each of you further into your own realities. Now you do not properly listen to what I say and if the proofreaders were reading that sentence they would change it to "you do not listen properly to what I say," but I mean you do not properly listen and there is indeed a difference. So while classes are formally suspended I want each of you to read our class sessions. There are hidden clues for each of you in those sessions and each of you know it and I want you to follow them. And the absence of our friends is a practical absence and yet it is also a symbolic absence. Symbolic indeed of an absence in the past and a journey of which you are all aware. And a journey you have in one way yourselves all taken. I have been speaking Sumari English to you all along. You use language like a fence and hide behind it. And if you will forgive me, we are giving you one quick boot and we will leave the sentence there so that you will not be able to use language as a hiding place any longer. You will learn to communicate and you will learn not to hide within the highly specific and inhibiting nature of words as you understand them. You throw them around like a ball in a game. All of you. But if you want to know what we are doing with the Sumari language, my dear cousin of Richelieu, we are taking away your ball and that is why you all feel so uneasy.

And suspense is the spice of life, so do not go looking for all the answers in one moment. You would be appalled if I gave them to you. I would be cheating you of the joy of your own self-knowledge. Some day each of you will say, "Aha, I understand. I have it." You may forget what you had but you will know that you knew the answers for a split second, and the tiniest cells in your fingernails will remember. Far be it from me to cheat you. I am indeed leading you on a merry chase. All chases are merry. But a chase is precisely what you need. It quickens your psychic blood and makes you think on your own and it makes you wonder why you do things. Why you will follow our Lady of Florence when she gets up and says we are going to make a circle, or why you would be kissed by our friend here, the cousin of Richelieu. Why do you do what you do?

Now we will continue with our circle. I mentioned once long ago that there would be some examinations in this class and since I have spoken those words many have come and gone, but there will be examinations.

([Bette:] "But on report cards, right?")

My dear cousin of Richelieu, you give yourself a report card that I would never give you. You are much harder on yourself than I would ever be.

(Molly Pearson said she had been doing this chanting for a long time.)

Do it some more and let yourself go when you are doing it and don't ask questions. Ask your questions later. Let yourself go with it.

Now you may have a Seth break and a Sumari break

and I'm sure Ruburt is ready for a class break.

(During break a discussion of the campfire scene and the sacrificing of a baby. Molly was commenting on Rachel's dream of space without objects and objects without space when Seth came through.)

As Ruburt would say, hold it. There are objects without space around them. There is space without objects. There is good without evil and this is simply the state of your understanding at this time. As such it is legitimate.

([Molly:] "In our reality we don't seem to know.")

In your reality you can, if you let go of the concepts. Now, I tell you, and I have told you many times, and regardless of how intellectually confusing it may sound to you in greater terms, there simply is no evil. And as long as you are aware of what seems to be evil effects then you are still in ignorance. Now there is space within objects and objects within space. Remember that. Now violence is a type of action and it is often misdirected. Whatever violence you did you did because you thought it was good and met a worthy end then; therefore, be careful of those ideas that you entertain now and what you will do to defend them. No one ever does violence for something he considers unworthy. The most bloodthirsty acts have been done because men believed themselves right and so they killed to uphold their worthy ideas. So be even playful with your ideas and what you believe, for no idea is worth killing for in your terms.

Now there was quite a bit more to that particular drama and it will come to you, and to you, and to you, and to you and to you and to you and to you and to you. And above all to you.

([Rachel:] "Were you there, Seth?

I was indeed.

([Rachel:] "At the campsite?"

I was at the center of the campfire and Ruburt was there in another guise.

([Rachel:] "Male?")

He was indeed.

([Rachel:] "Tall, thin.")

He lead you there at one previous class session.

([Bette:] "Seth, did I give her a drink out of a gourd? It was a split gourd and I offered her this drink before she had to leave.")

You did, indeed.

([Natalie:] "I was there as a young boy.")

You were.

Now what you have been and what you are, are as you know, one, so learn from what you are.

(To Arnold) And you have closed your mind to your own role, but we will get to it as far as our African god is concerned.

([Arnold:] "Was I involved in this episode?")

You were not involved in this episode.

Now you have also been involved in episodes that are not so bloody you see, but to you at that time these were not bloody episodes. They were intense encounters with good and evil as you understood them at the time and when you acted, you acted according to your terms of good and evil. Therefore, be careful of those ideas <u>now</u> that you entertain of good and evil.

(Bette said she felt a section of the campfire scene was missing.)

If I were you I would not ask.

(Sumari came through after break.)

Close your bones and listen to the timbre that creaks through your *(word lost)*. You have been in this room for centuries and while you sit here civilizations have grown together and blown apart. Listen with the part of you that does not know sight or sound. Listen with the part of you who knows… *(Word lost)*. You have been here for centruies and as you sit here in fleshy images so has the flesh come and gone and so are you free of it and independent of it and not surprised by it or astonished. It makes no impression upon you for it has come and gone. And so as all things that have come and gone already begun and in their beginning they change and alter, creativity once more arises and you play your part in it and you find yourselves embarked in a new world, in new sensations, in new encounters with self, even though the sense even now passes away and you know where the future is behind you and the past that is yet to come for the past is forever as new as the future and in all things are there beginnings without endings and even your ideas of endings rouse themselves and can never pass away. Now, as always, you are as eternal as you have ever been, as physical and as nonphysical, as real and as unreal. You are bony structures momentarily looking out through eyes and seeing through pulses, yet you form the eyes and the pulses and the worlds that make them possible and the dramas that so intrigue you from the past and the present and the future, and yet in all of these there are doorways, there are beginnings. There is *(word lost)*, there is knowledge and in all ancient things there are beginnings before births, there are images before thoughts, there are gods within gods, there are paths that you *(words lost)*. Your bodies are ancient. The bodies that you inhabit have come and gone. The minds that are your own are new. The selves are new but you have sat here for centuries, and in your aliveness springs the creativity from which all things are born and the joy and vitality that gives life to all worlds.

(After coming out of trance Jane described the feeling of being a skeleton.)

(Seth:) Be thankful for me because I am so fleshy. And so are you all. And when the Sumari come home *(to Rachel),* I would like it if they stayed home for awhile, which means that I would like to see you around for awhile.

([Bette:] "Was Rachel the waitress in this dumpy bar that you and I were in?")

I was never in a dumpy bar.

([Bette:] "Was she the waitress that was waiting on us at the table that I saw what you did the other night?")

She was the waitress and it was not a dumpy bar.

([Bette:] "And that is why she flirts with you in class, isn't it?")

It is one of the reasons

([Rachel:] "Our friendship goes further than that.")

It is indeed. It is of long standing and I expect to see

you around more.

([Rachel:] "As soon as I get a job.")

I will get you a job, then shut up. I will see that you get one, then you will have to play other games.

And now I bid you a fond good evening and I will keep my eye on you while our friends are away. When the cat is gone the mice will play.

([Florence:] "Keep an eye on Jane and Rob.")

I will keep my eye out for them also. Our friend is worried over here *(Rob)*.

Now I want you all, as Ruburt said, to reread the *Seth Material* and get out your questions, but more than that reread *The Seth Material* and imagine my telling it to you. And look out for those pieces of information that you missed earlier for they are important.

Now I bid you a fond good evening and I would wink at you but it is beyond my dignity.

THE SETH AUDIO COLLECTION

THE LATER SETH CLASS SESSIONS (1972-79) are not included in The Early Class Session books and are available on CD along with transcripts. These are audio CD's of the actual Seth sessions recorded by Jane's student, Rick Stack, during Jane's classes in Elmira, New York, starting in 1972. Volume I, described below, is a collection of some of the best of Seth's comments gleaned from over 120 of the later Seth Class Sessions. Additional later Seth Class Sessions are available as The Individual Seth Class Session CD's. **For information ask for our free catalogue or visit us online at www.sethcenter.com .**

Volume I of The Seth Audio Collection consists of six (1-hour) cassettes plus a 34-page booklet of Seth transcripts. Topics covered in Volume I include:
- Creating your own reality – How to free yourself from limiting beliefs and create the life you want, • Dreams and out-of-body experiences. • Reincarnation and Simultaneous Time.
- Connecting with your inner self. • Spontaneity–Letting yourself go with the flow of your being. • Creating abundance in every area of your life. • Parallel (probable) universes and exploring other dimensions of reality. • Spiritual healing, how to handle emotions, overcoming depression and much more.

ORDER INFORMATION:
The Seth Audio Collection Volume I. Send name and address, with a check or money order payable to New Awareness Network, Inc. for $60 (Tapes), or $70 (CD's) plus shipping charges. United States residents in New York State must add sales tax.
Shipping charges: U.S.—$8.00, Canada—$22,
Anywhere in world -$16 (Slow) $32 (Fast)

New Awareness Network, P.O. Box 192, Manhasset, NY 11030
(516) 869-9108 between 9:00-5:00 p.m. Monday-Friday EST

Internet Orders and Info **www.sethcenter.com**

Books by Jane Roberts from Amber-Allen Publishing

Seth Speaks: The Eternal Validity of the Soul. This essential guide to conscious living clearly and powerfully articulates the furthest reaches of human potential, and the concept that each of us creates our own reality.

The Nature of Personal Reality*: Specific, Practical Techniques for Solving Everyday Problems and Enriching the Life You Know.* In this perennial bestseller, Seth challenges our assumptions about the nature of reality and stresses the individual's capacity for conscious action.

The Individual and the Nature of Mass Events. Seth explores the connection between personal beliefs and world events, how our realities merge and combine "to form mass reactions such as the overthrow of governments, the birth of a new religion, wars, epidemics, earthquakes, and new periods of art, architecture, and technology."

The Magical Approach*: Seth Speaks About the Art of Creative Living.* Seth reveals the true, magical nature of our deepest levels of being, and explains how to live our lives spontaneously, creatively, and according to our own natural rhythms.

The Oversoul Seven Trilogy *(The Education of Oversoul Seven, The Further Education of Oversoul Seven, Oversoul Seven and the Museum of Time).* Inspired by Jane's own experiences with the Seth Material, the adventures of Oversoul Seven are an intriguing fantasy, a mind-altering exploration of our inner being, and a vibrant celebration of life.

The Nature of the Psyche. Seth reveals a startling new concept of self, answering questions about the inner reality that exists apart from time, the origins and powers of dreams, human sexuality, and how we choose our physical death.

The "Unknown" Reality*, Volumes One and Two.* Seth reveals the multidimensional nature of the human soul, the dazzling labyrinths of unseen probabilities involved in any decision, and how probable realities combine to create the waking life we know.

Dreams, "Evolution," and Value Fulfillment, *Volumes One and Two.* Seth discusses the material world as an ongoing self-creation—the product of a conscious, self-aware and thoroughly animate universe, where virtually every possibility not only exists, but is constantly encouraged to achieve its highest potential.

The Way Toward Health. Woven through the poignant story of Jane Roberts' final days are Seth's teachings about self-healing and the mind's effect upon physical health.

Available in bookstores everywhere.